IT MUST BE LOVE

THE JOURNEY CONTINUES ...

GRAM SEED

WITH ANDREA ROBINSON

CWR

In my forty-six years as a Christian, I have met only a handful of Christians who truly walk by faith. Gram hears that still small voice from God and obeys. Gram can relate in a very meaningful way to thousands of young men who are eager to find the answer to life and hear of the miracle of salvation that took place in his life in 1996.

Albert Dicken
Chairman of the Goshen Trust

Gram Seed's life story is inspirational for anyone who may be on the verge of giving up hope: it is the story of how God never gives up on us and it challenges us that we, the recipients of amazing grace, should never give up on others either. Gram is eloquent in sharing the story, and passionate about living it.

Lord Bates of Langbaurgh

Gram's story can best be described as a modern-day miracle. To those who have doubted their worth Gram directs his love and faith in God, reaching into lives with a message of hope and restoration. This second book is a testament to the commitment of Gram and his team of staff and volunteers and to God's faithfulness in changing lives for the better.

Sir Peter Vardy
Chief Executive of The Vardy Foundation

CONTENTS

FOREWORD

Gram Seed is on his way to becoming a national icon for ex offenders – although he would be the last to want or recognise such a status for himself. Following the success of his autobiography, *One Step Beyond*, he has now written this compelling sequel. It is a powerfully authentic account of his struggle to establish a ministry of loving rehabilitation on both sides of the prison walls in and around seven HMPs and YOIs in the North East and Yorkshire.

Although none of this trailblazing, and sometimes life-saving rehabilitation would have been pioneered without the leadership that has flowed from Gram's own remarkable conversion from criminality to Christianity, his new book co-authored with Andrea Robinson is essentially a story of God-inspired teamwork.

The team players are such an improbable squad that they could only have been brought together by divine selection. In the later chapters of the book, fifteen of them give snapshot testimonies of their own involvement with Sowing Seeds Ministries. Other senior supporters of the team, such as Brian Souter, Sir Peter Vardy, Albert Dicken, Lord Bates and the late Patrick Hinton, make cameo appearances in the early part of the narrative. All have been passionate enthusiasts for Gram's credo: 'Sowing Seeds continues to be about one thing: love in action. It is not just about saying the right words, but reaching out to those with broken lives; building up friendships, offering support, helping to show those going down the wrong path that in Jesus there is a better way.'

In the world of young offenders, the path of love in action

is never smooth. One reason why *It Must be Love* is a page-turner is because the bumps, the mistakes, the heartbreaking reversals and the cruel disappointments in Gram Seed's road are honestly chronicled alongside the life-changing success stories and the heart-warming examples of how the power of prayer can turn bad young offenders into Christ-centred good citizens.

This is a practical as well as a spiritual guidebook to offender rehabilitation. The gritty realism of its Northern experience reads far more convincingly than the political correctness of most Whitehall memoranda or Westminster speeches. And at every level of the story, the example and call of Jesus is the ultimate motivation for Gram Seed and his team. May there be many more followers on the same paths of *It Must be Love* rehabilitation in many more prisons.

Jonathan Aitken
Author, broadcaster, columnist, lecturer and campaigner for prison reform

INTRODUCTION

It was November 2008 and I was on my way to a mission event, when I received a phone call from CWR, the publisher of my first book, *One Step Beyond*. They were calling to invite me and Andrea, my co-writer, to a meeting to discuss the possibility of writing a sequel. I had been overwhelmed by the fantastic response to the first book, which had been published nine months previously, but the possibility of writing a follow-up had never entered my mind. However, CWR told me that many readers and booksellers had asked them how I was getting on and if anything else was going to be written about me.

I felt really excited about the opportunity – here was another chance to show people how the Lord can change lives, and also to show that He continues His transforming work. I was also excited that my story might inspire people to help others as I have done; my friend and mentor, the late Patrick Hinton, was prompted to set up Teen Challenge Teesside after reading a book by John Macey called *Tough Love*, about the beginnings of Teen Challenge. Teen Challenge is a Christian organisation seeking to help young people caught up in drug and alcohol abuse. I thought it would be awesome if one of my books had a similar effect on someone.

At first, work on the sequel was delayed; at the start of 2009 we were experiencing a freezing cold winter in the UK, and I was snowed in three times, unable to get to meetings! However, once I started my interviews with Andrea, I found them much more enjoyable than the times we had met to work on the first book. Two years earlier, when we were writing *One Step Beyond*, I had found it really painful to talk about my past. Often, when I drove home to Teesside after our meetings, I would be crying so much that I would have to stop the car. This time around, I travelled home rejoicing, having talked about everything the Lord had done for me until that point and how He had made my charity, Sowing Seeds Ministries, into what it is today. Reading the finished manuscript was really encouraging and emotional; seeing everything in print brought home the reality of the amazing things the Lord had done in my life and in the lives of others.

But there was one thing with which Andrea and I really struggled: finding a title for the book. We had had a few ideas, but none of them seemed quite right. Once, when Andrea came up to Teesside to interview other people for my book, we chatted about this issue. We talked about the possibility of using another Madness song title, and had a laugh about some possibilities – we didn't think anyone would want to buy a book called *Baggy Trousers*!

It was Chris Crossan, one of the lads I'm in contact with through the work of Sowing Seeds, who came up with the final title. As soon as he mentioned the song title *It Must be Love*, Andrea and I looked at each other, thinking the same thing: this could be it! I thought it was an awesome idea, but we decided to think and pray about it before finally making up our minds. A little while later, as Andrea and I were again talking about the book, the song started playing on the Sky Sports channel on a TV nearby – we were standing in a football complex at the time! We looked at each other and laughed. Was this coincidence or was the Lord trying to tell us something?

The more we thought about it, the more excited we felt. After we'd come up with the title, Andrea said that the writing of the book started to fall into place. It seemed the title said it all – it pointed to the amazing love of God the Father; to the love He gives us, the Sowing Seeds team, for those that don't know Him yet, and to the way that love has transformed so many lives. What was even more awesome was where the idea for the title had come from: a few months previously, Chris Crossan had been planning to commit a serious crime, when the Lord intervened in a powerful way. A man who had been about to carry out an act of hatred had later given us a book title about love!

I pray that as you read this book, you will learn more about this love that has changed so many lives. Whether you have been hurt or abandoned, have been through other difficult circumstances or are just curious to discover what life is all about and if what I say about the Lord is really true, I pray that you will learn as I have done 'How great is the love the Father has *lavished* on us, that we should be called children of God!' (1 John chapter 3, verse 1, italics mine).

The Lord bless you
Love
Gram

PART ONE:
MOVING ON

CHAPTER ONE

IT MUST BE...

As soon as I looked at him I loved him, and all my doubts disappeared. It was 5 May 2000 and I was holding my newborn son in my arms for the first time. At that moment something changed in me.

I had never known a father's love. My dad left when I was a baby, and I grew up feeling confused, rejected and angry. I was brought up on a rough Middlesbrough council estate with my mam, her parents and her brothers. There was love in my family, but sometimes I still felt left out and jealous of my uncles. I was ridiculed and bullied by other children because of my nana's mental illness, and I lashed out in anger. Part of my identity was missing for years, hidden behind masks of pretence, rebellion, crime, violence and addiction. This nearly destroyed me.

It was only when my life was transformed that I began to learn how to truly love. When I first *felt* this new kind of love, I thought something was wrong with me! I was not long out of hospital and was facing a lengthy rehabilitation, when I looked out of my flat window and saw some lads running over a bridge. I knew they were going to nick from the nearby shopping complex. I suddenly had a strange feeling in my heart and an urge to rush over and stop them. I panicked and went to find one of my friends – I thought I needed a psychiatrist! My friend told me the feeling would soon pass.

But it didn't, and on 9 November 1996 at 2.45pm, I found out what it was. I'd just asked Jesus into my heart. It was like nothing I had ever experienced: I finally accepted that someone truly loved me and believed in me. It felt like a burning joy, as if someone had given me the best compliment ever, but 1,000 times over. I cried real, heartfelt tears of happiness for the first time.

Four years later, tears marked that new revelation of love for my firstborn, Caleb. The Lord had already given me love for others – for the lads running over the bridge to commit crimes, for the ones paying for their crimes in prison, for my family and friends, for my beautiful wife Natasha – but now there was something different. I had worried for months that because of my past I wouldn't be able to love my child and be a good dad, but when I looked at him – wrinkled, crying and messy – all I saw was beauty. It was just as overwhelming when my second son, Boaz, was born three years later, in 2003. But when I became a dad that first time, something else happened. I finally experienced and understood God's love as a father for me. It began a new process of healing and growth.

I've dedicated my life to sharing with others the love I've experienced. From the moment I became a Christian, I was out on the streets where I used to hang around causing trouble, telling everyone who would listen that Jesus loves them. I had a real heart for lads in prison, where I'd spent so many years of my life, and God led me to set up a church-based charity to help them. I had a lot of supporters, but for a long time I was very much a one-man band, trying to cope with long, tiring days and driving hundreds of miles every week. However, God had something better planned; He wanted to bring a team together, independent of any one church, to reach those without hope. That's how Sowing Seeds Ministries was born.

While I was praying and fasting about this possible new

direction in my ministry, a man called Albert Dicken offered to fund a DVD about my life. A professional film company were hired and an actor was found to play the part of me – although he wasn't 6ft 5 and covered in battle scars and tattoos like I am!

Sowing Seeds Ministries officially began in April 2007, marked by the DVD launch at what is now Cineworld, Middlesbrough. So many friends, family members and dignitaries came along that the management at the cinema arranged for a large screen to be put up in the lobby for the overflow. This meant that members of the public going to see a film that night had the chance to see a different film for free – one about how the Lord can turn a life around.

As the lights dimmed and the film began, I felt overwhelmed. I'd sat in that particular theatre many times before, watching films with my sons, but this time we were watching my life story on screen. It was all there – the football violence, burglaries, scams, drugs, arrests, mental illness, prison and, finally, my three years living on a bench as a chronic alcoholic, before I collapsed and ended up on life support. If it weren't for those who had befriended me then, told me about the Lord and prayed for me, I'd be dead.

That night back at home, when visitors had left and Natasha and the boys were in bed, I was alone in our front room on my knees – the same place the Lord had given me a vision for the new ministry. Here I was again, a year later, but this time the vision had become a reality. In the silence I thought about the applause and the cheers that evening when the film had ended, and I was overcome with tears of joy and gratitude, praising God. The experience proved to me that with God, anything is possible and that my future is safe in His hands. It was time to start changing the future for others.

CHAPTER TWO

GROWING SEEDS

I'm rubbish at admin, and the Lord knows it! That's why He had to prompt me to read the email I was about to dismiss. I'm glad I did; it was the first indication that the next stage of the vision was about to begin.

I knew that the Sowing Seeds team was about to start coming together. I'd prayed for a number of roles to be filled, and one of them involved looking after the large amount of paperwork needed to run the charity. I was still trying to work alone and didn't have the time to deal with it all.

At first there wasn't enough money to employ anyone, but following the DVD launch, we started to receive more financial support. One of the supporters was Brian Souter, from the Souter Trust, who owns Stagecoach. I had met Brian during an Alpha supper at Sterling Castle, at which we had both shared our testimonies. He offered his support and gave the charity a generous donation that provided the funding for our first staff member. An email was sent to local churches advertising for an administrator.

The day before I was due to go on holiday to Butlins, I was at home pastoring a young lad called Matthew. I suddenly felt I should go and look on my computer, so I left Matthew in the kitchen, went into the living room and sat down in front of the screen. A new email had come through, and I glanced at it. Written in the subject line was 'RE: Administration'. I thought it was just a copy of the email advertisement being sent to churches, so I wasn't going to open it. But, in my heart, I knew I had to look at it properly. It was from a woman called Nina Dennis, and she was applying for the job. I felt prompted by the Holy Spirit to ring Nina straight away, so I did, and we had a long chat on the phone. Poor Matthew was still waiting in the kitchen – I'd almost forgotten about him! I knew from the Lord that Nina was the right person for the job, and she joined Sowing Seeds in September 2007.

It was such a massive relief to have Nina on board. Her dedication, administration skills and love for Jesus have meant that the ministry has run so much more smoothly since her arrival, and this has freed me up to focus more on what the Lord had given me to do.

As well as an administrator, we needed an office. Nina attended All Nations Church in Hemlington, Middlesbrough, and she asked the pastor there, John Ashwell, if we could use some of the church rooms as our base. He agreed, and after this things started to slot into place. We took on another office worker, Lynn Woodwark, who joined us part-time, and volunteers Liz Ashwell and Linda Wilson. This meant that by the time my book, *One Step Beyond*, was published the following year, we had a team in place ready to respond to the large volume of letters and emails that started to arrive from readers.

Once the organisational side was in place, I was able to focus on building a team to go into prisons. I'd previously visited establishments all over the country but, despite having more people on board than before, I decided it would be best to go for quality and not quantity, focusing our ministry primarily on some of the North East and Yorkshire prisons and young offenders institutions. These were:

- Hassockfield Secure Training Centre, County Durham – for 12- to 17-year-olds

- HMP and YOI Castington, Northumberland – for juveniles aged 15–17 and young offenders aged 18–21
- HMP Kirklevington Grange, Cleveland – for adults aged 21 and over
- HMP Holme House, Stockton on Tees – for adults
- HMP Northallerton, North Yorkshire – for young offenders
- HMYOI Wetherby, West Yorkshire – for juveniles and young offenders

As I prayed about my plans, I was contacted by Ian Williamson. Over the years, our paths had crossed a number of times. As we chatted, he told me he had seen on the Sowing Seeds website some of our ideas for the future of the charity and he believed God had given him the same vision. This helped to confirm that Ian should be part of the team. He was working as a school learning mentor at the time. We didn't have enough money to take him on, but I felt God would provide the funding for his salary. Ian believed me – and handed in his notice at the school!

Also around that time, I received a response from someone I'd been trying to contact for a number of years. Sir Peter Vardy is a former car dealership owner and has supported many Christian ministries. He's been involved in building a number of top-class schools in the North East with strong moral boundaries and a Christian ethos.

I'd been writing to Sir Peter for the previous seven years, asking for financial support for the work I was doing. However, that year I hadn't been in touch. That's when he wrote, asking me to come and see him.

When we met I told him more about our work and showed him the DVD of my life.

'It seems to me you need an assistant to help you,' he said.

'Why don't I put some meat on the bones?'

The money he offered was enough to provide Ian with a salary for three years. It blew me away. I thought I was dreaming when he told me what he was going to give, and it wasn't until we had received the first cheque that I realised it wasn't a dream. Sir Peter had got behind us in a massive way, and Ian was able to join Sowing Seeds in October 2007. It was further confirmation that we were on the right path.

At first I thought Ian's role might be to increase our funding by networking with churches and promoting the charity. But, when he started coming into Hassockfield with me, I realised how much the kids loved him and how well he fitted in. He also started going into Castington, and after just a week the staff gave him keys. He wasn't cut out to be what I was asking him to be.

'I think you should find your own job in the charity,' I told him.

Ian said he wanted to focus on the prison work and I agreed that he'd made the right decision. He also started to cover Kirklevington Grange, Holme House and some community and schools work.

Having Ian on board felt like me being in two places at once, especially as I wasn't allowed into Castington. I'd tried for seven years to get in – the same length of time I'd been writing to Sir Peter – because a lot of the kids from Hassockfield are sent there. I think the Lord had planned for someone else to take on the role, and I think Ian's work with young offenders will continue to grow and develop.

We also took on three more part-time staff members. Eric Young joined us as a football coach at Hassockfield and in various schools; Ben Falaja came on board to help in schools and young offenders institutions; and former pastor Brian Foskett was recruited to promote the charity, network with churches and encourage donations and support. Brian's daughter was one of the nurses who looked after me in James Cook Hospital when I came out of my coma. Brian started with Sowing Seeds as a volunteer going into prisons and wanted to continue working with prisoners when he took on his new role, so he could share his experiences when promoting the charity. We now also have two other volunteers, Harry and Gloria Holden, who have worked in Holme House Prison with offenders and ex offenders since 2007.

So, two years after the launch of the charity, we had three full-time and four part-time staff members, a team of volunteers, funding from Christian organisations and one hundred sponsors. It's been fantastic to see the way this has all come together. We have a lot of strong support now, and I believe God will bring more people and funding at the right time, as long as we make sure the charity remains 100 per cent Christ-centred. We believe that our Christian family will provide the support we need; the danger with funding from other sources is that it often comes with strings attached, some of which are not Christ-centred, taking our focus away from what the Lord has told us to do.

It will still take me a while to get used to my title as head of the charity – Chief Executive. I believe it was right to agree on this title, because I believe I should protect the vision, but it feels odd calling myself this – in fact, I had to write it down the other day and I couldn't even spell it! To me, it's just words and really I'm just Gram Seed, who heard of the Lord to do something. Anyway, I'm not really Chief Executive – I'm Chief Anything-That-Needs-Doing!

I know I don't need to control the team too much or order them around – that way is the way of the world. It should all be about Jesus having His way, not Gram. The Lord has told me I need to be the kind of boss who allows the team to find their own way with what He has given them to do, serving firstly out of love for Jesus and secondly out of love for me. They are getting on with the job and I trust them to let me know what's happening. I have the attitude that if I stay around something too long, I'll wreck it!

Even though I'm committed to doing what the Lord wants, I do sometimes get it wrong. That's what happened when we set up a halfway house for lads who had just been released from prison. I'd promised someone I was working with that I would find him a place to live on release. I approached the Goshen Trust, a Christian charity, who responded by buying a house in Eaglescliffe, over the road from a lovely park, and allowed us to rent it from them. We put two lads in on the understanding that they had to follow house rules about behaviour.

But it caused conflict in the community. Some of the neighbours were against the lads living there, and went to voice their opinion at an open meeting run by Safer Stockton, a group of professionals working towards reducing crime in the area. The residents complained that ex prisoners living in our halfway house had reduced the value of their homes.

Others spoke up in our favour – probation officers said they were glad we were able to spend time with these lads, more time than they were able to, and that if all those newly released were looked after in this way, Probation would have nothing to do. It was a very hard meeting. However, I was encouraged that those with the authority to stop the project were actually for it. The Lord had given us favour with the professionals.

But despite those in favour, the lads left of their own accord and we decided not to continue with the project for a while. We learnt that we should have employed a salaried, live-in house manager, because the rules were broken a number of times. We had a voluntary house manager, but he was unwell and the stress of the situation accelerated his illness, so he had to step down.

I took all the blame because the whole thing was my idea. I think I heard the Lord correctly about setting up the house, but I don't think I prayed enough about how the project was to be run. When I direct myself, I make mistakes. The mistakes I made in this case cost the charity a lot of money, but I did learn a great deal from the experience. I believe we'll try this idea again at the right time in the future, but next time we'll make sure we're better prepared.

Amazingly, the Lord turned my mistake into a blessing. A couple with five children were about to lose their home. They lived in a rough area – every night the dad had to sleep downstairs with a hammer because the risk of burglary was so high. The Goshen Trust offered the halfway house to this family, so now they enjoy a much better area, with really friendly neighbours, the park opposite the house and a great school nearby. The family are now a picture of health and are attending church. I think Jesus reached out to them and has made a beautiful life for all of them.

At the end of the day, despite mistakes made, Sowing Seeds continues to be about one thing: love in action. It's not just about saying the right words, but reaching out to those with broken lives; building up friendships, offering support, helping to show those going down the wrong path that in Jesus there is a better way.

This action has to come from the heart, from a genuine concern, because if you aren't sincere, people will soon notice. When I was an alcoholic, I remember going to see a counsellor. He said he felt he really knew me, liked me and believed I could sort myself out. However, the next time I visited him, he looked at his notes and then said, 'Hi, Paul, how are you doing?' I was just a file and a day job to him. Once the lads I work with are in my heart, I never forget their names and they are with me wherever I go, 24/7. It's not a job, it's a way of life.

Building on these relationships takes time, patience and hard work. You have to earn the right to speak into a person's life, and some of those we are reaching out to are very damaged. Suddenly, a big fat bloke from Middlesbrough (very good looking though!), turns up and says he's there for them and will be back next week. I have to follow through on this promise, building them up by loving them. Most of the kids I meet have never had this kind of consistency in past relationships, so often it can take months, even years, for them to start trusting me and opening up to me.

One example of this is Gary, who was in Hassockfield for police assault, burglary and criminal damage. I was asked to see him by the head social worker. Gary was very withdrawn and rebellious. I could see there was great sorrow in him. It was another five months before I found out why.

I didn't ask too many questions, but I prayed for him and became a friend. I played pool with him, had my dinner with him, listened to him and, as he grew to trust me, he told me his story. His parents had split up, but when they were married they used to run a pub together. Often, his dad would get drunk and hit his mum, and the police would be called. One night, when Gary was ten years old, he heard banging at the front door; his dad had turned up drunk again. Suddenly he heard a loud bang. Terrified, he hid in his wardrobe.

'Where are you?' his dad demanded. Gary stayed where he was, believing that as soon as he heard the police sirens, he would be safe. But there were no sirens that night. All he heard was another bang and then silence.

He finally crept out of the wardrobe, came out of his bedroom and found his dad's body on the landing and his mum lying by the front door. His dad had shot his mum and then himself. Ever since that day Gary had hated the police and blamed them for not being there to save his mum.

I worked with Gary for about a year and started to see changes in him. He gave his life to the Lord during Party in the Hack, the summer event we hold every year in the prison. He had been getting into a lot of trouble, but after a while his behaviour improved and as a result he was made an enhanced prisoner, which meant he gained extra privileges, such as access to computer games and longer telephone/visit times. He even began to write poems for me about being free. He was eventually released, and I understand that he went on to college and stayed out of trouble.

In some cases it takes a long time for people to change, but it seems God often prompts me to meet those who are on the verge of change. I remember one week when I wasn't planning to go into prison, but I had a feeling that I really ought to go. I was asked to see two lads, one from Manchester and one from Rotherham. They had both had horrendous pasts. The lad from Manchester, Craig, had been abused by an uncle and auntie. He had lived with his nana, who suffered from dementia, and was given no boundaries in life. He used to drink and take drugs. One day, when he was in this state, a friend jumped on his back, and Craig stabbed him.

The other lad, Pete, from Rotherham, carried a lot of anger, having been beaten up by several of his mum's previous boyfriends. As a result of this he got into fights.

Neither Craig nor Pete knew much about the Bible, and one of them couldn't read. I promised to get this lad the Bible on cassette, and he was really pleased about that. The second time I met them they asked how to become Christians. I prayed with them and they asked Jesus into their lives, and we started having Bible studies. They were both changing significantly. Pete went on to Castington and was later released. I don't think he's been back in prison since. Craig was released into a hospital for assessment, and has not been back to prison. I understand he was reconciled with his mum and went to live with her on her farm. He really wanted to be with her.

I find that a lot with these lads – they desperately want to be back with their mums. They are only children after all. Often, when they first come into prison you can hear them crying in their cells for their mums. I once wrote to the Home Office suggesting that if some prisoners were allowed to go home after a week, I don't think they would ever commit a crime again, because of the shock of going into prison. They come in desperate to go home, very withdrawn and tearful, but several weeks down the line they have become hardened to the system and the culture, and are fighting with staff and other lads. By that time, they have got used to it and simply follow the pack.

I may have the gift of the gab, but there are still times when I don't know what to say to the lads I meet. It's at moments like these the Lord gives me exactly the right words. There was one lad I knew about who had been taught by his family to fight, and he often assaulted the prison staff. I tried to approach him.

'I don't want to ——— talk to anyone,' he said to me and walked off.

I prayed about him. The Lord told me, 'Go and see him and I will give you the words.'

I made a point of going into the lad's classroom to speak to him. 'No hard feelings that you didn't want to see me, but the name's Gram, and if you ever want a chat, let me know,' I said, and then left.

A week later he wanted to see me and we became good friends. He didn't stop fighting, but the fighting was more in self-defence rather than attack. In another prison he broke his arm in a fight and stopped fighting after that. I don't think he's been back inside since.

Another time, I felt I was given the words to encourage a young lad who was really upset about being released; he had no mum or dad to return to, so was being sent to a care home. I was asked to see him, and he was in tears because he didn't want to go. I felt really troubled for him; what on earth could I possibly say to change his mind? Then I felt the Lord speak through me. 'I've got a plan for you, if you want it,' I told him. 'What you need to do is get out of here, get married, have kids and make sure your kids never get put into care.' I then talked to him about my life and my children.

Suddenly, he looked up and started smiling. 'That's it, that's what I'm going to do!' he said. He was ready to go then – his attitude had totally changed.

I believe the Lord gives me wisdom at moments like these. It's amazing – the Creator of the world chooses to speak to you and use you, even if some people think you're a bit wacky!

But that's what the work is all about, and when someone becomes truly free, my heart smiles. I was once a lonely, rejected teenager like many of those I meet, so it's a great relief when they choose another path. I can't change what I've been through and I still suffer some of the consequences, but I can use what I've learnt to reach out to others and stop them going the same way. And I was about to see that happen in a way that blew my mind.

CHAPTER THREE

IMPACT

It was the first book I'd ever read. I couldn't put it down, but I already knew it off by heart. It was my story.

It had taken a long time to get to the point when *One Step Beyond* was published. A number of times I'd been approached by people who wanted to write a book about me, but I knew the timing wasn't right. I had to be patient and allow the Lord to build strong foundations, to prove that my transformation was genuine and not just a passing phase. So, finally, after ten years of growth and preparation, here it was – my life in a book.

The only other book I'd ever read was the Bible. Reading had always been a struggle for me because of my lack of attendance and effort at school. When I became a Christian, I taught myself to read morning and night using a large-print Bible – because of my poor eyesight at the time – alongside Bible commentaries and Luke's Gospel on cassette. It was spiritual food for which I was desperately hungry, and I didn't want to read anything else. But, when I first started reading the manuscript of my story, I didn't want to stop. I found myself desperate to rush home, have my tea and get the kids to bed so I could read some more. If it had that effect on me when I already knew what was in it, how much more would it affect others? Pete Gray, from CWR, the publishers who produced *One Step Beyond*, told me that a bookshop manager he knew was so engrossed in the manuscript when reading it on a train one day, that he nearly missed his stop!

I was really excited about the opportunity, because I believed the book would be an awesome tool for Jesus. However, I was also apprehensive about what people would think of me. I had tried to honour the Lord by waiting to have a book written, and believed I didn't have pride in my heart, but didn't want people to think I was trying to be clever or trying to say I was something special because I had a book and a DVD out. I also worried that people might think it was rubbish and wouldn't want to read it.

But I needn't have worried. Since its publication in February 2008, literally hundreds have made contact to tell me how great the book is. It seemed to have the same effect on others as it did on me – once they started reading it, they couldn't put it down. There was something different about it. But most exciting of all, God had answered the prayer Andrea and I prayed right at the beginning of planning the book – that it would give people hope. It has given people hope in amazing ways, time and time again, and continues to do so. It has given hope to prisoners that a better life is possible, hope to their families that their loved ones can change, hope to professionals and chaplains in schools, prisons and probation that they really can make a difference. People have passed the book on to others, written to each other about it, talked about it around Teesside and, as a result, lives have been turned around.

What I found awesome was the way the Lord kept bringing the book into certain people's lives at exactly the right time. One local lad, Chris Crossan, who I mentioned in my Introduction, had a reputation in Stockton for being dangerous and mixed up with a lot of violence. He was on the verge of committing a serious revenge crime that would have meant a long spell in jail, when his friend gave him my book – his friend had just read it in two days in his prison cell. Chris broke down in tears as soon as he started reading it, and kept hearing a voice telling him to ring me. I met him and talked to him about the Lord and about what was behind his desire to commit the crime he'd been planning. Chris soon gave his life to the Lord and was baptised. He's since brought other lads to a group we've set up for new believers, has opened a gym called Redemption, to help other lads improve their lives, and is determined to turn his back on a life of violence and crime.

Another lad who contacted me after reading the book was Elliot. He was a tough bloke, from Crawcrook, on the outskirts of Newcastle. He had become a Christian about eight months before meeting me, but still had a serious cocaine addiction. I met him and his church minister, Clive. What blew Elliot away was that I'd just given a talk in Shrewsbury set up by a friend called Martin Smith. Martin grew up in my area and, while I was there, he'd been talking about this minister called Clive. It turned out to be the same Clive I then met, Elliot's minister.

'The Lord's gone before us, Elliot, and we're meant to do stuff together,' I told him.

We met up regularly, and one evening I went to speak at a youth project in which Elliot had some involvement. Around fifty really rough teenagers came to listen. When I gave my testimony, they were as quiet as mice and asked loads of questions. I hadn't planned to hand out any copies of the book, because I had thought a lot of the teenagers coming that night wouldn't be into reading. But I really felt the Lord prompt me to give out some copies. I got out a box from the car, handed the books around and had a coffee with Elliot before I left. As I drove down the main street of the town, I couldn't believe my eyes – there were all the kids I'd just spoken to dotted along the road reading my book! Some were on the ground, others were in bus shelters or on walls, totally engrossed in the story. I was amazed at the Lord's power and was absolutely buzzing, wanting to go back and talk to the kids, but there wasn't time. The kids have asked me to go back again.

I really wanted to get *One Step Beyond* into Borders bookshop in Teesside. I was buzzing when it happened because there were already a lot of books there on crime in the area, focusing on local gangster and football violence – and there was mine in the middle of them all, talking about hope. It meant that many people in the area who knew me from the past were able to buy a copy. One person who did, approached me at a football match, when Middlesbrough were playing Wigan.

'Flippin' 'eck, Gram Seed!' he said. 'I've just read your book and it was brilliant! I've read all the other books and they are a load of rubbish, but yours is awesome – there's something different about that book.'

'There is. It's Jesus,' I told him.

'Oh, I don't know about that, Gram, but there is definitely something about it,' he said, and shuffled off.

Football's been a part of my life for many years. In the past, I'd only go to matches to beat up the other 'firms', the opposing team's hooligan gang, but nowadays they're a wonderful opportunity to tell people about what Jesus has done in my life. And five days a week I take my boys to Power League in Stockton, where they have pitches for kids to train and play. All the staff there have read my book. One of them, Paul Midgley, really feels that something's happened to him since he read it. He said it's an amazing story that has really touched him. I gave him a bracelet with 'What would Jesus do?' on it, and he's never taken it off, not even in the bath!

Someone else who's read the book has known me since I was thirteen. She said it stirred something inside her and made her feel 'spooked'.

'That's the Holy Spirit in your heart – there's no ghost,' I told her.

Her son is going off the rails a bit, and when she finished the book she sent him a text, telling him she loved him – she realised she hadn't said that to him for some time.

The book has also encouraged professionals dealing with offenders and those on the verge of exclusion from school. A lot of police officers who knew me as I once was, have read the book and are very supportive of the work of Sowing Seeds. One of them, Brian McCarthy, had previously put me away. He has since become a Christian and asked me to baptise him. An ex con baptising a copper speaks volumes to lads in prison. Brian is now Teesside's representative for the Christian Police Association and has received permission from the Chief Constable to put copies of my book in all the police cells in Cleveland.

Twice now I've been invited to speak to student police five weeks before they go on the streets – many have read the book or watched the DVD. They ask questions about how to get alongside someone who is like the old me. I tell them that there's always a bigger picture than the one they see at first. The lad screaming at them on the street is really saying 'Help me', but we don't always realise it when faced with such conflict. A lot of people, professionals included, have found my story a real eye-opener. They hadn't known how bad I'd become, and they had no idea about my dad or that my nana was ill. When all this came to light in *One Step Beyond*, it made Gram Seed seem more real to them and explained a lot of my behaviour.

The book has also opened more doors into schools. We at

Sowing Seeds particularly wanted to work in schools where there were kids on the verge of exclusion, and since the publication of *One Step Beyond*, we've had more invitations to visit these sorts of schools. RE teacher Penny Barker, at Conyers Secondary School in Yarm, Stockton, read the book and now invites me into her school to speak to new starters in Year 7, who undertake a project on my life. All the children read the book, watch the DVD and ask me questions. This arrangement was once featured on the local BBC news programme. My wife Natasha was chatting to some other mums at a regular meeting she goes to, and when she told them my story, they said it sounded familiar. It turned out that their children went to Conyers Secondary School and now their mums were reading my book too. Ian Williamson's stepdaughter Hannah, who's seven, has also done a school project on my life and gave her teacher a copy of my book.

There are a lot of coincidences like the ones I've mentioned, that I like to call 'God incidences'. My sister-in-law, Cathy, who is a Christian, told me that one lad at her church suddenly seemed different, somehow happier. She asked him what had changed.

'I've been reading this brilliant book,' he said. 'I can't remember the title, but I'll bring it in – you've got to read it!' It was my book, and he was amazed when he found out Cathy is my sister-in-law.

But there was one person whose reaction to the book I was really nervous about: my mother, Pat Lawson. She's always been a very strong woman, especially while I was growing up; abandoned by my dad, looking after her brothers and the home while my nana was ill, having to work long hours and having to cope with my behaviour. I didn't ever want her to feel bad about my past and to think that she was in any way to blame. In addition, the bad things about to be published about her son might put her family in the limelight.

She didn't read the book for months, but when she did, she said it was brilliant; she cried, she laughed and she was happy about what was written. She read it again, and thought it was even better the second time around. She also lent it to her friends, who were blessed by it.

Not everyone in my family has commented on the book, but Denise, my uncle Terry's girlfriend, said it's the best thing she's ever read in her life. She also told me that she had miraculously recovered from having very bad headaches after a car crash. They were so bad that she used to collapse and fall downstairs. Despite having tests, lumbar punctures and MRI scans, doctors couldn't work out what was wrong. One day, I visited Denise and Terry and, as I left, I asked her if she still had the headaches. She said they were still really bad. I simply placed my hand on her head and said, 'In the name of Jesus, don't let Denise have any headaches ever again.' It was very simple and quick. She hasn't had a headache since, and that was five years ago. She was chatting to Natasha one day, who was telling her that the Lord was real. She said, 'There must be something there because our Gram prayed for me and I've never had a headache since!'

I really hope this is the start of the Lord having an impact on my family. When I first became a Christian, my uncle Terry said, 'Well, I believe in evolution.' Rather puzzled I said, 'Oh well, good for you!' The truth was, I didn't even know what evolution was! But none of them can deny the truth of what's happened to me, and some have started to support the work I do. My brother-in-law Lance, who's a bit of a tough cookie and not a Christian, was really touched by the book and offered to pay for some to go into prisons.

It's been fascinating to see the places *One Step Beyond* has gone – Buckingham Palace, for example! Doreen, a lady from our church, sent a copy to the Queen and received a reply. She's also sent them to Prince Charles, Jack Straw and to churches in Tenerife. And it's gone even further than that – it's now being sold in Australia. One woman there contacted me, thinking she might be a distant relative.

It's also been translated into Arabic. Clarion Publishing House in Beirut, a charity that distributes Christian literature, asked for permission to translate the book, and CWR have given them funding to produce 2,000 copies.

One project I have been particularly delighted to be involved with is The Torch Trust, a Christian organisation for the blind. They had *One Step Beyond* translated into Braille and an audio version produced as well. I was invited to record the introduction to the audio book so that those listening can hear what I sound like; I understand that blind people particularly like to hear an author's voice.

The exciting thing is, you never know where the book is going to land and who's going to read it. Someone might be reading it at this moment and find that hope and strength in Jesus that I and so many others have. But one of the most thrilling results is the way the book has affected lads in prison.

Before *One Step Beyond* was published, CWR put out an appeal for funding to supply the book free to prisoners. After a tremendous response, they were able to print 20,000 books, and they received requests for copies from more than 100 prisons all over the country. Pete Gray from CWR contacted me and asked if I was OK with this happening.

'Are you kidding?' I said. 'That's absolutely awesome!'

It wasn't long before the letters started coming in. At the time of writing this, we must have had close on one hundred from prisoners all over the country. Many of them felt when reading the book that I was speaking directly to them, because their lives were so similar. I'd been where they were and was 'one of them', rather than an outsider with no understanding. Because of this, they were more likely to believe that what I was saying was true. One example of this was the case of a lad called David. He was doing a life sentence for murder along with his brother Carl, and he read my book while in solitary confinement.

'Carl, you think Jesus does love us, like this lad's saying in the book?' David shouted to his brother, who was in a nearby cell.

'He's one of us, why would he lie?' his brother replied. The questions continued, and the next morning, it was still on his mind.

'I just keep wondering whether it's true or not, this Jesus thing,' David shouted to his brother again. That night he went to bed and said out loud: 'I wish I knew whether it was true or not, what this lad's saying. Jesus, I wish I knew You loved me and that You are real, 'cause I just want to die right now. I can't manage this sentence.'

The next day a volunteer visited the prison and spotted David's name on the board listing inmates.

'Oh, I've got a message for him from someone called Mary, who used to take him and his brother to Sunday school when they were children,' he told the chaplain. Mary had heard that the brothers were in prison and told the volunteer that if he ever came across them, he was to give them a message: 'Jesus loves you.'

As soon as David was given the message, he put his hands in the air and said, 'I know now that You're real!'

A lot of lads in David's prison have now read the book, and I was invited to go in and meet them. The first planned visit was cancelled, but I believe this was in the Lord's timing because when I eventually went, David had started attending one of the chaplain groups, and couldn't wait to tell me his story.

'I was ready to kill myself because I was facing thirty-one years in prison for something I didn't do,' he told me. 'But now I feel free. I'm going to protest my innocence until I get a retrial, and I know justice is going to be done.'

A lot of lads claim to be innocent. I don't always know whether or not they're telling the truth, so I always tell them to keep praying about their situation and remind them of the importance of the truth, because it is the truth that really sets you free. But even though David might be in prison until his sixties, he was buzzing and had a huge smile on his face. And David's brother had noticed the change in him.

Often I'll come across lads in prison I knew years ago, who have read the book. I had a letter from someone in Frankland jail who was doing a life sentence – he was part of a family I knew well, and I'd started praying for this man the first morning I became a Christian. He wrote that he had got a lot of hope from the book, which meant a lot.

Once, when visiting HMP Whealston, I met some lads from Middlesbrough who knocked about with me when I was a skinhead. They told me the book had really spoken to them because they knew the areas in it and can now see some light at the end of the tunnel in their lives. They have gone to chapel more since reading the book. They've been honest and said they don't want to become Christians, but they don't want to commit crime any more. It's a start – a step closer to God's kingdom.

Another local lad who read the book in prison was Cliffy. He was with me when I collapsed and went into a coma, and he phoned for an ambulance for me. I met Cliffy again after he had been released from prison, and he told me that the book had really touched him, especially as he had witnessed first hand a lot of the events in it. In prison he had started going to chapel groups and writing to people about the book.

It's awesome the way the Lord has used the book to open doors into more prisons. One lady, who organises prison missions, was struggling to find a speaker for HMP Kilmarnock. She prayed about it, and someone gave her my book; after reading it she felt prompted to invite me to speak. I gave a talk in the chapel at Kilmarnock, which was bursting at the seams with about one hundred lads. When I asked who wanted to invite Jesus into their lives, nearly all of them put up their hands. On another occasion I visited HMP High Down in Surrey, and eighty-nine lads who had read the book came to the chapel that Sunday. I was warned that I would lose them after ten minutes, but half an hour later, I was still talking and they were still listening. I felt prompted to ask if any of them wanted to start attending the prison Bible study – there was a huge queue to sign up.

I often find that those who have read my book are encouraged to do what I'm doing. One lad, Paul, a heroin addict, read my book at HMP Risley. After he was released, he came to hear me speak in Manchester and approached me afterwards.

'I went to the chapel in Risley, gave my life to Jesus and I'm striving to be like you, Gram,' he said.

'Remember, it's Jesus, not Gram Seed, who makes the difference,' I told him.

And it's not just male prisoners who have been touched by my story, girls have been too. Hassockfield has a section for sixteen girls. I go and visit, but always with a staff member present. This is a bit restrictive because the girls don't always relax and open up about things when staff are there. I feel it's best that I focus on working with the lads, but one day I think we'll have a lady on the team who can work with girls.

I was, however, once invited to visit Downview, a women's

prison next door to High Down in Surrey. As I was praying about the day early in the morning of the visit, the Lord told me I was going to see a tall girl with long hair, who had bad teeth because she'd been on crack cocaine. He told me to tell her that the Lord was going to fill in the gaps in her life. When I arrived, she was the first girl I met, and she was in the chapel with the others as I shared my story. During a question time afterwards, I looked at this girl and said, 'You don't know this yet, but Jesus wants you to know that He's going to fill in all the gaps in your life – the Lord told me that at 6am this morning.' Suddenly she was crying, and said, 'I really hope so, because that's what I want.' Everyone in the chapel started cheering and clapping – they must have known something about her that I didn't. In fact, they cheered and clapped every time one of the girls said something positive. I hadn't come across this before, and I encouraged them to continue supporting each other, especially on the wings (the prison sections where the cells are).

After the meeting, I spoke to the girl again. She was thirty-six, had been involved in drugs and prostitution since she was a child and had been in jail nearly all her adult life.

'We need more people like you to mentor others,' she said.

'Why don't you start something?' I replied.

'Who, me?' she looked shocked. 'How could I do that?'

'Ask Jesus to help you.' Suddenly she was crying again, but this time she was also smiling. She had found a purpose in life. And more than that, for once someone had believed in her ideas rather than telling her that she was worthless scum with no education.

After this, the chaplain of Downview, Rosie, contacted CWR to let them know that a lot of the girls were now regularly attending the chapel and one, a Muslim, was going along to every chapel service she could.

One Step Beyond has also helped many families of prisoners. Some lads pass the book on to their dads, who know me from the past. Sometimes prisoners' family members are affected more than the prisoners themselves. All new lads at Hassockfield get a copy of the book and one of them, Kevin, sent the book to his mum. He told me she had cried when she read it.

'Do you know why she cried, Kevin?' I said.

'No,' he replied.

'It's because she loves you and the book gave her hope.' He was really moved by that. The week after, I went to see Kevin on his release day, and his mum was there. She recognised me straight away and was crying as I talked to her.

'Keep believing there is hope,' I told her. 'Don't give up.'

Another lad at Hassockfield read the book and told his nana and granddad about it. His grandparents are strong Christians and his great granddad was a Methodist preacher. The lad's nana wrote to the prison a few times, trying to locate me, and when I found out, I contacted her and sent a copy of the book and the DVD. She was really encouraged when I told her that her grandson's behaviour had improved, and found great comfort in knowing I'm there for him.

At Hassockfield, new social workers get a copy of my book so they know who I am, and other staff have read the book. One worker, a care officer, read the book twice. Once was while he was on holiday, and he lent it to four other people around the swimming pool. He said my story opened his eyes and that he'd like to attend Bible studies to find out more.

When I wrote the book I had a feeling prison officers would read it, and I wasn't sure what their response would be. However, at one book signing day for the lads, a lot of prison officers asked for signed copies as well. So many said the book was brilliant and gave them another perspective on prisoners. I was blown away by that.

I'm sure the book has helped chaplains as well. Being involved in prison ministry is a gift from the Lord, but there are many disappointments to be faced; it is easy to lose heart. Hopefully my book has given some chaplains the encouragement to carry on. What I have learnt in my work is that it's vital to stay close to the Lord and ask the Holy Spirit for His help all the time. It is also important to ask for a lot of prayer and other support from the wider church.

I had mixed feelings about prison governors reading the book, because it contained information about their prisons; I was worried they might stop me visiting their institutions. However, I've found it's encouraged more of them to invite me in, especially into 'Category A' jails, the most secure type of prison. Before, it had been very difficult for me to access these places. There are some lads in these prisons who had asked for my support, and now I am able to get in and see them.

The book has gone before me and helped to give me credibility in the eyes of governors and other prison staff. Once, a prison contacted the charity and asked if 'Mr Seed' would come in. I'd never been called Mr Seed in my life – only in court! And then they sometimes skipped the 'Mr'!

One Step Beyond has led to fantastic opportunities to reach out to so many people, and I've been blown away by the response. Writing it took hard work and brought to the surface a lot of emotional pain; it added another demand to an already busy schedule and I often used to cry after talking to Andrea about the terrible things I had done. Being thrust into the limelight isn't easy and does have its down sides, but it's meant others have been blessed and I have had many memorable experiences – some of which I could never have imagined.

CHAPTER FOUR

COMPLETE MADNESS

As a sixteen-year-old skinhead, they were my heroes. If anyone had said to me that one day they would be reading a book about my life, I'd have told him he was off his head!

When I first met the band in a Camden Town pub, they were called The North London Invaders. They were young kids like me and were just starting out in the music business. I thought they were brilliant and said hello to them after they had played the first part of their set. But it was a rough pub and a fight broke out. A lad had a bottle and I thought he was going to smash Suggs (Graham McPherson) with it, so I pushed Suggs out of the way. Stopping fights wasn't my usual behaviour – I was normally in the middle of them throwing punches – but I thought Suggs was a good singer, and if he was injured we wouldn't get the second half!

I continued to follow the band closely over the years, and when they became Madness I saw them in concert many times. The most memorable concert was at Newcastle City Hall. Carl Smyth, known as Chas Smash, looked into the crowd, pointed in my direction and shouted, 'One Step Beyond!' Well, that did it! In a flash, I was up on the stage with them, jumping around like a madman, doing the Moon Stomp, which was a rather crazy dance that looked as though you were leaping around on hot coals. The Lord must have had a good laugh about that one, knowing what was to come in the future! The band members didn't mind – in fact, they had a dance with me – but the bouncers weren't happy. They dragged me off stage and threw me out of the building, but I sneaked back in through another door.

But it was the hit song 'You're an Embarrassment' that I really identified with. It seemed to sum up everything about my life, even though at the time I didn't really care what effect I had on people.

When Andrea and I wrote *One Step Beyond*, Andrea contacted Madness's management company for permission to use the song's lyrics in my book. They kindly agreed and asked for copies of the book for the band, which I signed. I kept in touch with them, and received a VIP invite to see a concert they were doing in Birmingham and to meet the band. I turned down the invitation. Now everyone thought *I* was off my head!

I had already agreed to visit a prison in Norwich that day. I could have gone there for a bit and then travelled to the Madness concert later in the evening – and I really wanted to – but it would have meant cancelling one of the talks I had planned to do that night, and I didn't want to let the lads down. I'm glad now that I didn't go to the concert, because nine kids at Norwich gave their lives to the Lord, and many are still going strong in the faith.

'You should have gone to the concert. Think of the missed opportunity and the publicity you could have got for the charity,' I was told. But I believe in the Lord's timing. I knew I would have another chance.

That chance came in December 2008. I had felt prompted to invite the band to perform a charity concert for us in Teesside. I thought it would be a fantastic thing for the area, and I hope we might arrange for it to happen in the future. The Madness management sent VIP invitations – this time to attend a concert in Manchester. I didn't hesitate.

I arrived early, with my friends Sammy and Dean, to meet the band before the performance. Backstage there was a spread of complimentary food and drink and there were a lot of people milling around, also waiting to talk to the band. We were told the band had been a bit delayed.

When Suggs and Woody (Daniel Woodgate) arrived, they recognised me straight away. 'We know you; you're that man with a changed life that we've been reading about!' they exclaimed.

Chas Smash, who has always been one of my favourites, was the last of the band to appear because he'd still been getting ready for the show. He had long-distance family visiting that night who he hadn't seen for years, but he managed take a few minutes to chat with me. He told me he'd read my book by the pool while on holiday.

I told Suggs about the time I first met him, in Camden Town as a teenager. He said he vaguely remembered.

And, of course, I didn't miss the opportunity to tell them about Jesus! 'You've met the man in the book now, but you can meet Jesus too, and He will make your life more complete than it is now,' I said. 'In fact, it's complete madness to live a life without the Lord!' *Complete Madness* is the name of one of their albums, so they had a good laugh about that. They were very open to what I was saying. In one of them in particular, I could see deep pain and sadness. I've continued to pray for him.

I had photos taken with Madness and watched the concert – they've definitely still got it! It was a really special evening and such a blessing from the Lord. I often have a laugh about how it all came about. Who would have thought my hero band as a teenage skinhead would end up meeting me and reading my book; I could never have planned it. It's a real testimony that if you follow Jesus with all your heart, He'll fulfil your dreams. I know that all my dreams have come true.

I don't make a habit of mixing with famous people, but I've been in the spotlight a great deal since I became a Christian, because of the dramatic change the Lord brought about. I've been in newspapers and magazines and on radio, TV news programmes and video. I've even been in a comic strip! I was featured in the first edition of a Christian magazine called *Cops and Robbers*. The magazine contains stories of criminals changed by God, but in comic strip form for those who struggle to read. Copies of *Cops and Robbers* are put in a lot of custody cells. CWR bought the rights of the strip about me, and now produce it as a stand-alone comic.

When *One Step Beyond* came out, the publicity increased. I travelled to different parts of the country to promote the book and undertake signing sessions, often facing long queues of people wanting me to sign their copy. Once I visited the Spring Harvest event at Skegness, spoke in the Big Top and was interviewed on stage for Premier Radio by Jeff Lucas – he was weeping as I told my story. That night, I didn't start signing books until 11.30pm, and there were around 300 people in the queue – I was still signing two hours later.

It was awesome that the Lord was using my story – and very humbling – but all the publicity felt rather odd. It also led to a few unexpected adventures. Once, I travelled to London to do a live broadcast on Revelation TV. Ten minutes into the programme I was supposed to be on, I was still rushing to get to the studio! I'd actually arrived at the location an hour earlier, but I wasn't sure I was at the right place. It was a large house and had no signs on it to indicate what it was. It looked nothing like a TV studio – more like a dentist's surgery! I rang CWR and was given another possible location, which I quickly drove to. I then received another phone call to say I was right the first time, so I set off the way I'd come. It was close now to the time I was meant to be on. You can always guarantee that it will be at times like these that the volume of traffic will triple, all the lights will turn red and old ladies will decide to cross the road! Ten minutes after the 9pm broadcast time, I arrived, was rushed inside to what looked like a back bedroom, and plonked on a chair in front of a blue screen. I'd not had a chance to get a meal that evening, so was starving hungry, and there was the cameraman sitting in front of me eating a Chinese meal! I answered some questions from callers and got back to the hotel tired and grumpy. To top it all, my sat nav had taken me through the congestion zone and I was charged £60.

Back at the hotel I still didn't have anything to eat – it would have been too expensive. Next morning, I'd planned to meet former MP and government minister Jonathan Aitken, who had read my book. He bought me a massive breakfast.

I'm always a bit of a stickler for punctuality, so I hate being late. I had another close shave when I was chatting to someone on the Tube and nearly missed a visit to the Houses of Parliament! I had been invited to the fiftieth anniversary celebration of the Langley House Trust, a Christian charity that supports ex offenders. The trust founder, Roy Calvocoressi, had invited me after he had attended my DVD launch, so it was a real honour. Travelling to Westminster on the Tube, I started talking to a man sitting across from me, and began to tell him my life story. He seemed really interested, but my stop was coming up. I had a dilemma: should I stay or should I go? In the end, I decided to carry on talking to the man and to get off at the next stop. But, when I came out of the Tube station, I turned the wrong way and ended up even further away from Westminster. Time was running out – I needed to get there quickly. I had £5 sandwich money in my pocket, but I had to spend it on another Tube ticket. I arrived at the Houses of Parliament twenty minutes before the event was due to start – stressed and hungry once again!

It is a huge place. There was a meeting in the House of Commons the afternoon of my visit, so there were police and security teams everywhere – travelling up and down the Thames in boats every twenty minutes, stationed inside every room, patrolling with guard dogs. I felt really uncomfortable, standing around in my one and only suit, which didn't fit any more because I'm too fat! Everyone was staring at me as if I wasn't supposed to be there.

The event itself took place in a building next to the Houses of Parliament known as the Conservatory. It was unbelievably posh, even the toilets! There they had paper towels as soft as handkerchiefs and luxury perfumed soap.

Back in the main area, the waiters were serving odd little nibbles – tiny bits of bread with meat and cheese on top. I only tried one; it was pointless having any more – I'd need at least thirty to fill me up! Plus, I had a nice lunch to look forward to … or so I thought.

The whole thing wasn't really my cup of tea – I couldn't wait to get out and get back into my normal clothes. I'm not really a suit person – I felt like I was trying to be someone else. But I was hungry. Then it was announced that lunch would be delayed until 2pm. I was leaving at 1.30 – another missed meal. Thinking of the too-tight suit, I think the Lord's trying to tell me something!

But getting lost, delayed and misdirected can often lead to some good opportunities. Once, when I was travelling down to CWR, near Farnham, Surrey, I wanted to turn off the M1 to find a toilet, but roadworks meant I had to wait and pull off further along and use the toilet at a pub. In the bar, I bought a blackcurrant and soda and a bag of nuts. Suddenly, I was surrounded by football fans, swearing and getting drunk. I went into the toilet, and by the time I'd come back, another thirty people had appeared. The whole group were looking at me rather threateningly – they had heard my accent and knew I wasn't one of them.

'Where are you going then?' one of them demanded, glaring at me.

I told him I was going to a book signing at a church.

'Book signing? Church? What are you on about?' More of them were crowding around now. I started telling them that I was a Christian and told them about my book. By the time I got up to leave the pub, loads of them were asking for books. What started off looking like a dodgy situation ended with me telling some fifty football hooligans about Jesus!

The mistake I've made a few times is not to have books with me all the time. I get chatting to people, and so often they want a copy. I always carry them with me now.

On another occasion, I went to Ireland with CWR. The plane back, from Ireland to Newcastle, was cancelled, so I had to fly to Manchester instead and then take the train to Middlesbrough. Once on the train, I spoke to Nina on the phone, and told her about something I was going to pray for. The man sitting next to me overheard.

When I'd finished my call he said, 'I heard you talking about praying – are you a Christian?'

I told him I was, and we got chatting. He was a lecturer in architecture and attended St Michael le Belfry Church in York.

We decided to keep in touch, and he told me later that he'd mentioned our meeting at his cell group that night and loads of people had said they knew me and had heard me speak. He later contacted me and invited me to be involved in Summer Soul, an outreach event in York. I gave a couple of talks, and this resulted in about fifty people re-committing their lives to Jesus and fifteen giving their lives to the Lord for the first time.

On another occasion, I bumped into Lord Bates, a Conservative Party peer, in an airport shop. I was on my way to give a talk in Guernsey, and was flying from Newcastle to Exeter. We both bought bottles of water and then got chatting as we waited for the same flight. Once we'd boarded the plane, he came and sat with me. Moments like this still stun me. There I was, someone who used to live on a bench, sitting and having a chat with a lord! We've become good friends since.

I get recognised in many places, and people approach me and start chatting. It happens when I go out with my family – when we go shopping, when we visit the cinema or when we go on holiday. It once happened at Euro Disney! I was with my family and my mam, who had treated us to the trip, when someone stopped and pointed – not at Mickey Mouse or Donald Duck, but at me!

'Look, it's Gram Seed! You did an Alpha course and it was brilliant. We became Christians on it.' Everyone was staring at us by now.

'We can't go anywhere!' said my wife, Natasha.

It's been fantastic to have had so many opportunities and to meet all those who have been inspired by what the Lord has done in my life. However, people's reaction to me isn't always so positive. There's a negative side to being in the spotlight. Some are watching me for a different reason. They are waiting for me to fall.

CHAPTER FIVE

SUSPICION

I'd been a Christian for about a year when I received a worried phone call from my uncle Terry. I'd been spotted on my bench, clutching a bottle of White Lightning.

'I'm really disappointed in you, Gram,' he told me. 'You're back on the drink again, aren't you?'

A lot of people thought this would happen. I'd been in such a bad state, then suddenly I appeared to have completely transformed. They doubted me, and it was fair comment; I had thirty-two years of baggage to deal with.

But as soon as I woke up from my coma, I knew I'd never touch a drink again. So, when my uncle called and told me what had been reported to him, I cracked up laughing.

As soon as I became a Christian, I was out on the streets every day talking to people about Jesus and I helped on the Teen Challenge bus on Fridays.

One evening, I'd gone to 'my' bench and met an old drinking friend there, Jimmy Leadbetter.

'Hey, you – what are you doing on my bench?' I said. We had a bit of a laugh and chat.

'Do you want a drink, Gram?' he said, offering me his bottle of White Lightning.

'No thanks.'

'You're not still on about that stupid Bible thing, are you?'

I talked to Jim about it again and told him that Jesus loved him.

'I'm busting for a wee. Hold that for me,' he said, thrusting his bottle into my hand and dashing off. One thing an alcoholic never does is put his drink down; it could be knocked over or some of it spilt. Drink is precious – but it wasn't precious to me any more. I looked at the bottle I was holding and took a sniff. 'How on earth could I have drunk that?' I thought to myself. It was at this point my uncle's friend drove past in a taxi.

I don't think my uncle believed this story when I told him.

There were lots of rumours going around about me. Five years after I had left hospital, rumours were still going around the town that I was dead!

Another rumour that went around had to do with a time when I was seriously tempted to venture back to one of my old haunts.

It was a Friday evening and I was heading out to the Teen Challenge bus. It was pitch black outside my flat because the local kids used to regularly throw stones at the streetlights and break them. Suddenly I spotted someone waiting for me in the shadows. It was Darren, a recovering alcoholic and heroin addict who'd not long been out of jail. He rented a flat near mine and had got a job with his brother-in-law at ICI, earning £700 a week, cash-in-hand – a lot of money, especially back in 1997. I had very little money at the time; I was able to save £5 a week, and at the end of each month I would use the money I'd saved to buy a sweatshirt, pair of jeans or something like that.

'Gram, do you want to come to The Millennium with me?' Darren said, offering me £50 spending money. The Millennium was a nightclub, just five minutes' walk away. The battle began in my head: 'One night won't do any harm,' I thought. 'I haven't been to a nightclub for ages; I've got some nice clothes and new aftershave. I haven't had a kiss off a lass for ages either. Or a dance, and I love dancing. I could just have a drink of orange, couldn't I? What harm would it do?'

But I soon came to my senses. 'No thanks, I'm off,' I said, and started walking away as fast as I could. The thoughts were still in my head, though: 'Go on, it's all right, Gram. It's just once. What about your new shirt?'

I was walking faster and faster to escape, and ended up jumping on a bus to get me there quicker! As soon as I arrived at the Teen Challenge bus, I felt relieved and happy. In reality, I don't think going to the nightclub would have been that bad, but I didn't want to risk it because I might have felt other much worse temptations along the way.

I wasn't out of the woods, though; Darren was outside my flat again the next week, it was almost like an action replay of the previous incident. This time he smelt strongly of drink – he'd just downed a bottle of wine. He told me he was waiting for his girlfriend, but I didn't believe him. Once again he offered me £50 to go out with him. This time it was much easier to say no. I trotted off down the dark road, praising the Lord and praying in tongues really loudly. The Lord had helped me to resist the temptation and I felt so happy. But someone was watching me.

'What are you doing, Gram? Are you all right?' A girl I knew came up to me. I later heard she'd gone into town and told everyone that I was walking down the street shouting about Jesus and talking to myself in a funny language.

'Aw, poor Gram. He's ill – that's probably what's been wrong with him,' people responded. So that's how the rumour started that I was brain damaged!

For a long time I was watched by so many people – friends, family, police, probation officers and security guards. I was often under surveillance and followed around town; it was like being on *Big Brother*. My mam managed a hotel for many years, and at one time I used to steal from the till behind the bar. Even as a Christian, for a long time all eyes were on me when I visited her. Gradually, trust built up, and I remember the day when I realised she saw me differently. I was visiting the hotel with my friend, Patrick Hinton, a wonderful, godly man who supported and mentored me for a number of years until his death. Patrick and I had a meal together, and afterwards I told a staff member that I was going to say goodbye to my mam.

'She's already gone,' I was told.

'Flipping heck, Patrick – she went without saying goodbye. Why would she do that?' I grumbled in the car on the way home.

'Don't you get it, Gram?' he asked me. 'She's that comfortable about you and trusts you so much that she forgot you were here!'

I rang my mam that night to say thanks.

'I didn't say goodbye – you and Patrick must think I'm really rude!' she said.

'It's OK, Mam. You trust me now, don't you?'

One of the hotel's former staff members who used to be told to keep an eye on me, married a vicar and recognised me on an Alpha video; up until that point, she had no idea that I'd changed. I gave a talk at her church, St Martin's in Hull, and she told everyone there the story of me robbing the till one night when she'd gone out back.

As a new Christian, I was anxious to show people that I had changed, but wasn't sure how to do this. I came up with one solution: a large gold cross on a chain, bought from my mate's jewellery shop. I wore it around town for about six months. Patrick tried to drop hints that he thought it was a bad idea by saying things like, 'Oh, here's the archbishop!' when I appeared. But it was the Lord who helped me to understand; one morning during my prayer time, He said, 'You don't need to have that cross on, because I live in your heart.' I told Patrick and he said he'd tried to tell me the same thing. I gave the cross to a family I know. My life, not my jewellery needed to speak about the new me.

And even though many prison staff now believe my story, it took a long time to convince them it's true. This is understandable – I'd spent so many years inside, fighting and generally causing chaos. It took a miracle for me to start being allowed access to prisons – ex offenders aren't normally allowed back. I was tested on many occasions, and prison officers often did everything they could to wind me up. They would search me thoroughly – for a while on every visit – take away every item I would have with me, search every pocket, check the soles of my shoes and threaten to strip-search me. They would call me names such as Speed, because I used to limp – I still can't walk fast. But not all of them treated me this way. One thing the Lord told me early on in my Christian life was that I'd caused conflict in the prison and police canteens, because some believed I was a fake and others stuck up for me.

In the face of opposition like this, I need to try and display a Christlike attitude. This is what I tell the lads in prison to do when they have a hard time with the officers. I remind them that they don't always know what is happening in prison officers' personal lives: one may be dealing with his wife leaving him; another may have had a kid die. They shouldn't allow it to affect their work, but sometimes it does.

Mind you, I haven't always followed my own advice! Sometimes I would get angry about the way I was treated by prison officers. At Holme House I've lost my temper and had to go before the governor. Everyone laughs about this, because when I was in there as a prisoner I went before the governor once, but as a Christian I've been before him twice! The first time was after I'd sent a £10 postal order to a Christian lad so he could phone his daughter on Christmas Day – he hadn't been in touch with her for twelve years. I did this through the chaplain, but I'd said it was from me personally, which was viewed as suspicious. I should have sent it from the church charity I ran at the time – Emmanuel Prison Ministries.

'You've got to be whiter than white, Gram. You are under a microscope right now,' the governor warned me. 'There are some officers who don't want you here, but I want you here.'

When I told people about this afterwards, I got my instruments mixed up. 'The governor told me I'm under a telescope!' I told everyone.

The second time I went before the Holme House governor was after I'd tried to film the front of the prison for a DVD presentation. I was at the entrance with my camcorder, when I realised the battery was dead. I decided to try again the next day, and so went to put the camcorder back in the car. Suddenly, two prison officers came flying over.

'Give us that camera, now!' one shouted.

'The battery's dead. I couldn't film anything,' I told them.

'We want it now!' They were really laying into me, shouting at me in front of everyone around. I lost it.

'Here, mate, I didn't allow you to speak to me like that when I was a prisoner and I'm certainly not going to let you speak to me like that now. You can get lost!'

'We know where you're going,' I was told.

'Where?' I asked.

'Not in there! You're barred for the day.'

'So where are you going now?' I said. 'I bet you're going to go to the governor and lie.'

They threatened to report me, so I phoned the governor

on my mobile. The officers ran into the prison as fast as they could.

The governor's busy with meetings and not normally in his office, but he was there that day. 'You should have just left it, Gram, and not lost your temper,' he told me.

I said the whole thing would be on the CCTV tape, and asked if the main governor in charge of the whole prison could look at it. I went to see him the next day and he said he could see both sides of the story. He said that if I ever wanted to take pictures or film anything, I just needed to phone up and ask first.

After this incident, I made a point of finding the officers concerned and saying sorry to them, because my attitude wasn't that of Christ Jesus. At the time, one of them didn't want to know, but he's fine now; the other shook my hand straight away and said it was fair enough.

Occasionally, a prison officer I'd known when I was a prisoner will be allocated to one of the prisons where I now work, and will wonder what on earth I'm doing there. They will wonder why I'm walking in through the staff door instead of the prisoners' one. This rarely happens now – I'm known about and part of the furniture.

Sometimes I've found that it's not only officers who are wary of me but, surprisingly, it's also chaplains. Many have welcomed me and are really grateful for my input, but some have been disinterested or hostile towards me. As I've said before, being a chaplain is a hard job, and there are many disappointing situations to deal with. It's easy to get worn down. I understand that some ministers might not get on with me because I turn up at their prison, where they have slogged away for years, and suddenly lads start giving their lives to the Lord. I hope that I can learn to work with them better, and that together we can show God's love to lads inside.

I can understand why non-Christians who knew the old Gram are still suspicious of me. However, I have, unfortunately, found that some Christians, despite seeing me grow in the Lord, have questioned my calling. When I wanted to leave the security of working with a church and receiving a regular wage, to start Sowing Seeds, some weren't too sure about it. One church leader took Natasha aside one day and asked her if she thought it was a good idea.

'I trust Gram – he's heard from the Lord,' she said. 'I came from London to support him 100 per cent, and I'm going to stand by him.' It blew the bloke away. I think he thought I was somehow cocooned and naïve.

Since then, I've heard of some people who question my actions not because they think I'm naïve, but for the opposite reason – they think I've got a scam going. I've heard that some wonder where I get my money from, as I have a nice house and car.

On another occasion I was hurt when I heard someone say that it was not possible to 'make it' in the church I attend, Tees Valley Community Church, because 'Gram's got top spot'.

What hurt the most about hearing these comments was the fact that I thought these people knew me.

When *One Step Beyond* came out, and with all the publicity surrounding it, the critics were there again. People made comments such as, 'Oh, you're a celebrity now, are you?' Others said, 'Oh, I bet you made some money out of that, you must be minted now.' The truth is, Sowing Seeds made a bit of money, but I asked to be paid in books, and I give most of them away.

The Lord also showed me that some people would read the book and mock it because it's about Jesus and a whacky head-banger tramp who was all over the shop, in and out of prison and is now a Bible-basher. I could understand why. Addicts were waiting to tell me that Christianity didn't work because they were frightened to have a go themselves, in case it failed for them. Even though my life has become more peaceful and theirs less peaceful, they still deny the evidence.

Looking back at all this I can now see why the Lord made me wait ten years before writing my life story. If your foundations aren't deep enough, being in the limelight could either hurt you or go to your head. If I took any of the credit, I'd be robbing Jesus of the glory, and I'm not a thief any more.

What I do takes constant commitment and sacrifice. The Lord woke me from that coma for a reason, and I take what I've been called to do very seriously. If I want to see people change, I've got to put the work in. That means getting up early every morning, sometimes as early as 5am, for prayer and Bible study. In the early years of my Christian life it meant I was out on the streets every night, doing a lot of things for the Lord that I didn't always tell people about. For instance, for the first two years after becoming a Christian, three nights a week I used to cycle around my estate, praying for the area (I also thought it would help me improve my health after being in a coma). After a while, I noticed things happening, for example, there were more raids on drug dealers in that time I was praying, even though I hadn't directly prayed for this to happen. I knew the Lord was moving.

As well as the opposition from people, at times it's been physically hard for me too. My health isn't good. The discs at the bottom of my spine have worn away over time, which causes me constant pain. I had to have two days of rehabilitation in hospital to learn how to cope with the discomfort. I have pain in my knees because of too many years living in the cold – the problem I suffer from has never been diagnosed. While living on my bench I suffered frostbite, which has killed the nerves in the bottom of my feet – when I walk, it feels as if I'm walking on exposed bones or like trying to walk on your hands using just your knuckles. I can't walk without shoes on, and if I stand on the smallest thing or walk on flat surfaces it's like someone sticking knives in my feet.

The Lord was gracious enough to heal me of partial blindness, but all the other pain I suffer has been with me since I woke up from my coma. I don't talk about it very often, but I live with it every day. I think the Lord gives me the grace to cope, but I don't know why He hasn't healed me completely. Often I think that perhaps the problems are the thorns in my side that keep me real.

I work on the frontline of Satan's camp every single day, and come under attack in many ways. Those of us who work in these sorts of positions need a lot of support and prayer from the Church. Natasha and I have a few friends, but not loads – many people assume the opposite because I head up a charity and have released a book and a DVD. Our family doesn't live nearby, so we don't have their help when the children are sick, or have babysitters when we want to go out. I often worry that my wife is not supported enough when I'm away, and she also faces prejudice because she's from the South. I love what I do and I'm passionate about it, but I think it's important to point out some of the difficulties so that people can support and pray for us and anyone else they know in a similar role.

But one important lesson I've learnt over the years is that I don't have to stick up for Jesus. I used to get angry when people mocked my faith or wouldn't believe, but the Lord has taught me that it's not necessary for me to do so. Once I was having a debate with a lad about Jesus when, suddenly, I stopped in my tracks and said, 'You might be right.'

'What?' he said. He was a bit stunned.

'Well, I'm not God, am I?' And that was it; I stopped talking to him. I sensed that I shouldn't be arguing for the Lord when He can look after Himself. My job is to be faithful in telling people about Jesus, and then to allow them to choose whether they want to follow Him or not.

If you've got a powerful testimony, some people will put you on a pedestal and others will try to knock you down. I have to strive to keep humility and love as my foundations, and to remember why I'm doing what I'm doing; I'll never forget what the Lord saved me from, and there's a lost generation out there in desperate need.

CHAPTER SIX

THE FATHERLESS GENERATION

'I hate you!' my son Caleb shouted at me. It was like a knife in my heart. I'd been disciplining him about his behaviour.

He was only young at the time and hadn't been talking long, so maybe he didn't understand what he was saying to me. But his words were still painful to hear. For a while, I really believed that he didn't love me any more.

I was thinking about this incident during my prayer time the next morning, when the Lord spoke to me.

'That's how I feel,' He said. It was then that I began to understand for the first time the depths of grief God the Father experiences when we, His children, rebel. He sought to save us by allowing His own Son to be sacrificed for our sins, and it hurts Him when we reject His love, guidance and strength. And when we turn away from biblical principles, we suffer the consequences. We join the fatherless generation.

So many times now in my ministry, I have felt some of the Father's grief. It breaks my heart – as it does our heavenly Father's – when I see those I've tried to help reject the Lord and fall away, even those who seemed to have been making good progress. I know what sort of life they are going to have without the Lord – I've been there and I know the pain they are going to go through.

It's especially painful when I know these people and their families well. One story I will never forget is that of

Liam, and the tragedy of his life. Liam was one of a family I'd known for years, and was like a nephew to me. In fact, I sometimes used to help look after him and his nana's son, who were the same age – they were really good friends. At one point, I hadn't seen the family for about four years, but I knew Liam had gone to prison.

One day, I was visiting Holme House and a lad said to me, 'Isn't it bad about Liam?'

'What about him?' I said, puzzled.

'He's dead!'

That couldn't be right; Liam was still in jail as far as I knew, and he was only twenty-one. He'd been in Castington Young Offenders Institution. I had planned to go and see him, but my visits kept being cancelled. Then he was moved into Acklington – a place I'm not allowed to visit.

The lad told me that Liam had not been out of prison long when he went out drinking one night and also took some sleeping tablets. He'd died of an overdose. Sometimes lads get things wrong or tell you stories that aren't true, so I had to find out if what this lad had said about Liam was right. I did a bit of detective work to find out where his mam and nana were living. I went round to see them and as soon as I got there, his auntie flung open the door and threw her arms round me, crying.

'It must be true then, eh?' I said.

They took me into the front room, and there was Liam, lying in a coffin – the young kid I'd known since he was born. He had been dressed in his favourite track suit and baseball cap and was wearing his gold jewellery; his family had placed all his money in his hands. He had been such a good looking lad – 6ft tall with everything going for him – and here he was, cold and lifeless.

I heard that there had been some strange things going

on at the house before I had arrived. Some Christians who had been involved with the family had turned up and commanded Liam to get out of the coffin. I was a bit upset about this because they had done it in front of the family, which I thought was tactless. But the truth was, I didn't want Liam to be dead either, and I prayed that if it was the Lord's will, He would bring Liam back to life; I wanted it so much for the family. I really struggled with this, as I had done in the past when so many others I had known had died. But there, sitting alone in the room with Liam, I remembered what preacher Smith Wiggelsworth had once said: 'Man is in a great place when he has no one to turn to but God.' That was me. I had nowhere else to turn, no real answers.

The great comfort in all of this was that I believe the Lord told me that Liam had made his peace with Him in prison. Apparently, Liam had watched my DVD in Castington, and some of the lads in the group said they didn't know if my story was true or not. Liam had stood up and said, 'That's my uncle and I can tell you that everything he said is true.' I also know that his nana told him to say his prayers every night.

I visited Liam's family every day until the funeral, at which I was asked to speak. Out of the fifty funerals I've been to, I've spoken at forty-five, but this was by far the hardest one. Praying the night before about what I was going to say, I realised I'd been given a great responsibility. There were going to be so many people there – friends I'd grown up with, many who weren't Christians – and I wanted so much for them to hear the Lord and experience His comfort.

On the day of the funeral, I felt very alone because I'd been distant from the family for a long time and wasn't really part of their lives any more. I trusted the Holy Spirit to help me speak, but it was so hard to hold back the tears and I think I got in the way a bit. But I managed to tell them that

I believed Liam was with the Lord. I told them about Liam watching my DVD in prison and telling the other lads there that my story was true.

I stayed on at the cemetery until everyone had gone home. It all felt like a re-run of Michael's death. Michael was a lad I'd known and cared about since he was seven – one of the lads I'd seen running over the bridge the day I first felt the Lord's love. Michael died of a drug overdose when he was twenty-four, and his death devastated me. At his funeral I had sat by his graveside in tears after everyone else had left.

Liam's grave was in a corner of the cemetery, next to a public road. I drove my car near to the grave, parked and spent about an hour there, praying. The Lord spoke to me from Hebrews chapter 13, verse 5: 'Never will I leave you; never will I forsake you,' and I finally began to feel peace.

When I think about tragic deaths like Liam's and Michael's, I have so many unanswered questions. But, although death seems like the worst thing that could happen to our friends and family, we can never know what the Lord might have saved them from, or what is around the corner for us. I just keep praying that the Lord will bring good out of bad situations and heal those who have been hurt.

Liam had a dedicated and loving mother, but his dad had been in and out of his life. I believe he grew up without a stable male role model. I've seen this repeated so many times – this is the other tragedy of the fatherless generation. Nearly every person I know in prison grew up without his or her dad around. I was like them – on the estate where I was brought up, it was normal. Nearly all children in my neighbourhood either lived with their nana, auntie or mum, and the dads were either occasional visitors or had disappeared altogether. That was many years ago – the statistics for today tell us that the situation has become much worse.

One of the first effects on those whose dads have left is experiencing feelings of rejection. Others I know felt this same feeling when they were young. I never met my dad, even though he lived in the same area as me when I was growing up. I used to see other dads visit their children and couldn't understand why mine didn't want anything to do with me. I thought it was somehow my fault that he'd left, and I blamed myself for a long time. Gradually, over the years, the feelings of rejection and guilt, along with other issues in my life, grew into a boiling rage. As a result I behaved really badly, and had to face the consequences of that behaviour.

As well as feeling rejected, the lack of a good father figure in a child's life can also mean they grow up without being made aware of certain boundaries. Of course, many single mums do a great job on their own, but I believe that a dad can help and support a mum, and can offer a certain firmness when teaching children, which they respect. It's hard for a mum to support a family *and* teach and discipline the children. Without a dad's influence, kids can end up rebelling, as I did, and can sometimes wrap their mums, nanas and aunties around their little fingers. My granddad tried to be a strong father figure for me, but when he died, his influence died with him, and my behaviour got worse. Any child is at risk of going down the wrong path. Even though my own children have been brought up in a Christian home with mum and dad around, if I let them, they would wreck the house, eat every sweet in sight, drink every can of pop, smash windows and steal. In a less stable environment, kids are at more risk. The lads in prison don't know the meaning of fatherly love and have never experienced any loving discipline. They often laugh about what they've done wrong and don't fully understand the consequences; it was just a bit of fun and they happened to get caught.

Kids who don't have strong dads around can grow up desperately searching for role models and can end up following the wrong ones – celebrities leading immoral lives, local criminals and gangsters or other members of their peer group. They will follow and copy what their 'heroes' do, no matter how crazy. My granddad summed up this sort of behaviour well when he challenged me once: 'If that man wore a toilet on his head, would you? Would you think it was fashionable?' I think there are some that would do this!

I try to be a friend to these lads, but also a good role model. I feel that the Lord has put fatherly love for them in my heart, which is about so much more than being a mate. When I show them fatherly love and teach them the difference between right and wrong, they start changing from withdrawn, naughty kids to positive and better behaved kids with smiles on their faces.

But it's not just the kids who are affected when a dad leaves; the mum who is left behind to care for the kids suffers too. Relationships break up for many reasons, but what is always certain is that the woman will feel pain. She may feel hurt or abandoned, but has to carry on looking after the kids, and it's likely she'll face financial hardship. A lot of ladies seem to suffer from guilt – they blame themselves for difficult situations even when they are innocent victims. Patrick Hinton once supported a girl who'd been sexually abused for eleven years as a child. When the truth had come out and her abuser was imprisoned for twelve years, she came to see Patrick in tears.

'Why are you upset about this?' he asked her.

'Look what I've done! I've told the police and he's had to go to prison for a long time,' she said.

'But it's not about what you've done,' Patrick reassured her. 'It's about what he did to you.'

Many ladies seem to carry a similar burden, believing that if they had done things differently, they wouldn't have been hurt or abandoned – or seen their children affected. Before he ended up in prison for bigotry, my dad used to hit my mam and steal money for drink. Making a stand against him and not allowing him back into our lives was one of the best things my mam ever did. But she still felt guilty sometimes for the way I had turned out, even though it wasn't her fault.

Women aren't doormats, and I believe the Lord wants them to be treated with respect. The man is meant to be a good role model for his children, and if he can't be that then he'll upset the whole house. Ladies need to be strong in these sorts of situations. But they also need the love and healing of their heavenly Father. Time is a great healer, but so is Jesus – He will help these ladies more than any man will.

I was saying this to a lady who found herself without a man, and she said: 'I know all that, Gram, but what I really want is God with a bit of skin on.' When a woman is lonely, it can be so easy for her to jump to the first man who comes along, because she wants a replacement husband or a dad for her children. Often, the first thing a lad in prison will tell me is that since his dad left, his mum has had five boyfriends. Sadly, in the past, I've often been one of the boyfriends of ladies like these. There are men who think a woman on her own with kids is easy meat, and often both the woman and her children end up being mistreated. These ladies have often been through a lot already, and it has taken them a long time to learn to trust again.

It's sometimes easy for an abandoned woman to believe that the first man who shows interest has been sent by God. However, he could end up being just as bad as the absent dad. In these situations, it's important to be very wise. I have a lot of admiration for my mam for waiting ten years before marrying her current husband. She tested the water and made a great choice. She's with a lovely man now who treats her well and she's really happy.

If you have been left by your boyfriend or husband, trust the Lord and get right with Him. He'll show you what He has planned for your life, which includes bringing the right people into your life at the right time. I often refer people to Jeremiah chapter 29, verses 11–13. Verse 11 says: '"For I know the plans I have for you," declares the LORD, "plans to prosper you and not to harm you, plans to give you hope and a future."' But this needs to be backed up with verse 13, which says: 'You will seek me and find me when you seek me with all your heart.' You need to know God the Father first and focus on building up a strong relationship with Him. Then He will meet your needs. I'm close to some Christian sisters who have lost husbands and they all say the same thing – that Jesus becomes everything to them: someone to love them, to be their friend and to meet their needs.

And your heavenly Father will also help you to spot those men that are trouble, like a loving dad faced with the old Gram!

'Dad, I'm seeing Gram and I want to bring him home.'

'You are not! That boy's trouble and you are not having anything to do with him.'

The Lord is a wise and protective Father who will teach you to discern things – to work out if the man treats your children well, whether he really values you or just wants to sleep with you and disappear, and whether he is trustworthy and reliable.

The other benefit of having the Lord in your life is that you can have a Christian family to support you, if you get involved with a good church. They can warn you about risky situations; in fact, they will usually go to great lengths to warn you if someone is not right for you. In prison, if a lad has done something wrong on the wing, other prisoners will break their necks to tell you about it. If someone is making advances to a lady on her own, her church family can help her discern whether or not that person is right for her, so it gives extra security and protection.

A mum can also pray for protection for her children, that they will not suffer any ill effects from having an absent parent, and she can know her children are safe in the Lord's hands. The children in a single-parent family need the Lord's love and guidance just as much as their mum, and Jesus will fill the gaps in their lives left by the absent parent.

This makes a difference if a mum remarries. If I had had a relationship with the Lord from a young age, rather than focusing on myself, I might have appreciated that it was important that my mam was happy and with someone who treated her well. She found that someone, but I hated him because I thought he was taking my mam from me, leaving a gap in my life. If that gap had been filled with Jesus, I would have acted differently.

Sometimes, though, if a dad is still on the scene and has rejected the Lord and biblical principles, it can have a negative effect on the family. It seems now that in many cases there have been three generations of absent dads. Many dads today weren't disciplined by their dads, and their dads in turn were not disciplined. When faced with fatherhood, many men today can't cope with the pressure and responsibility. They don't know how to be dads, so decide it's easier to abandon the family. They need the Lord to teach them how to be good dads and good husbands. Sometimes the faith of a wife can draw a man to the Lord. But often men don't like it when their wives are right – I think that's why a lot don't become Christians! But the Lord is faithful. I know one woman who kept praying for her husband for sixteen years – he went to an Alpha meeting and got saved. Now husband and wife work together with the homeless.

The change has to be in the Lord's timing. Even as a Christian I didn't become a good dad overnight. It took me many years to work through the issues I had with my own dad. As an angry, drugged up teenager, I had got to the point where I was looking for my dad in order to kill him for hurting my mam and abandoning me. I found out only recently that it wasn't just me and my mam he hurt, and he ended up dying a lonely, painful death as an alcoholic, suffering from cancer. It wasn't until I decided to go to his funeral that I was finally able to forgive him and repent from my attitudes of bitterness and resentment. It was then that the Lord released me from the spiritual hold my dad still had over my life – even after his death.

When Caleb was born, I had to start learning from the Lord how to be a good dad. It took years to get it right. When I first started the prison ministry I was on my own, trying to do about nine different jobs, and my family suffered. I didn't realise at first, but gradually I began to feel that something was wrong and knew I was under stress. I do what I call a spiritual MOT every three months. I read the Bible books Colossians and James, which remind me how to live as a Christian. Once, when undergoing this process, I realised that I was putting the ministry before my family. I needed to make sure I was being an effective leader with the vision the Lord had given me, but I also needed to change my focus. Now I make sure I'm available to take the children to school, that I get home at a reasonable time in the evening and spend time taking my children to football and the pictures, which I love doing. I can still work on the phone and witness when they are playing football, but we're also spending that time together as a family and it helps us to grow stronger. There's no substitute for making time for your children.

Family life is not without its difficulties, as any parent knows. Caleb, who's nearly nine, has dyspraxia, which can affect his motor skills. In 2008 he was also diagnosed with ADHD, which means that he kicks off sometimes. The strain of all this can be tiring for Natasha, but I believe in the Lord for his healing.

Caleb's development is helped by football, and he's training at Newcastle United Development Centre as a goalkeeper. This helps to make him more content and his co-ordination has come on really well.

Both my sons are Christians – Caleb has been filled with the Holy Spirit and speaks in tongues. They love the Church, and Caleb sometimes travels with me and speaks to the congregation.

I know the Lord, my Father in heaven, loves my children more than I ever will be able to, and He will look after them, but because we come under a lot of spiritual attack, my children are probably more badly behaved at times than a lot of others. But I would never pressurise them to behave for my sake. If I'm ministering to someone, I'm no less anointed because my children are misbehaving. All I can do is teach them, as guided by the Lord, and allow them to make their own decisions in the future and hopefully avoid some of my mistakes. I remember only too well the heartache my behaviour caused my mam. At one stage, it got so bad that she offered me money to get out of her life for good.

'You're worse than your father ever was!' she told me, as she disowned me. She was right – I was evil. It came back to haunt me when I lived as a tramp on a bench and I would drink to get rid of the pain. I would be devastated if my boys ever treated their mother like I treated mine.

The pattern may well have continued to the next generation if I hadn't have met the Lord. If I'd become a Christian as a child, I wouldn't have become addicted, got tattoos, gone to jail, become disabled, been forced to live with the consequences and the physical pain. But the Lord is using my mistakes to prevent others treading the same path.

The sad fact is that there are so many in this fatherless generation that don't know who they are, where they have been or where they are going. When I met the Lord I knew who I was, where I had been and where I was going – all at the same time. I may not always have influence over absent parents and be able to prevent them or their children making wrong choices, but I can show them the heavenly Father. It's only the Lord who can heal broken families and damaged lives, and stop the pattern of destruction continuing to generations yet to come.

CHAPTER SEVEN

BACK TO THE FUTURE

'What a bunch of idiots,' I muttered to myself as I watched in disbelief. I'd been flicking through some TV channels when I came across a programme about football violence. Drugged up Dutch hooligans with bald heads and no shirts on were dancing wildly and snorting coke at a late-night rave. Suddenly it hit me and I sat back in my chair, stunned. 'That used to be me!'

The Lord has brought me a long way since the days when I was one of them. I'm still surrounded by reminders of what I used to be, but other things have changed over time; old friends have died or moved on, and groups I was once part of have disbanded or have shrunk – I understand that The Frontline, the 'firm' I used to be part of, is now a small-scale gang called TS1.

Some of the places where I used to hang out no longer exist as they once did. In fact, one of my regular haunts, the Masham pub, is now a sports shop. I remember being in there, surrounded by crowds of lads and lasses, wearing my Armani suit and crocodile skin shoes. I often laugh to myself about this when I visit the new shop to buy sports gear or trainers; at one time I was doing deals and getting drunk in what is now their stock room!

But I also remember standing outside that pub as an alcoholic tramp covered in dirt and vomit, crying as I replayed that same scene in my head. I couldn't believe how far I'd fallen.

There was one very significant object from my past that I thought would always be there. For a year after becoming a Christian, my bench was the first place I went to every night while out on the streets and the last place I visited before returning home. I met a lot of my old drinking mates there and told them about the Lord. Sometimes I would just sit there thinking about how my life had changed. But one day, after I had married Natasha, I went there as usual and the bench had disappeared. In its place were some metal posts for tying up pushbikes. They didn't even ask my permission! I was gutted. I knew it was just a bench, but for three years it had been my whole world and my home – I even gave it a garden, courtesy of a flower tub I nicked from a nearby McDonalds! But as a Christian, the bench had become symbolic of the freedom I now had, and it kept me real. I know it sounds daft, but if I'd had the chance, I would have bought the bench from the council and kept it as a reminder. But it's long gone now.

There are things I still don't fully understand about my previous life, but often the Lord reveals answers in His own time, sometimes when I least expect them. One of the unanswered questions I had was to do with my dad's behaviour. I'd forgiven him for what he had done in abandoning my family, and had repented of my anger and bitterness, but I still didn't understand why he did what he did and also didn't want anything to do with me.

After *One Step Beyond* was published, I received a text message from my half-sister, Tracy. I'd first come across Tracy at my dad's funeral. My aunt had pointed her out, but I didn't really think anything of it – I had only gone to the funeral to face issues to do with my dad, not to meet my extended or step family.

When Tracy sent me the text, she told me that her husband had bought her my book in Borders, and she asked if I would like to meet. I hesitated because I didn't have a lot of spare time. But, after discussing it with Natasha, we decided we should both go and meet Tracy. We arranged to meet her, her husband and their three daughters in Brewsters, in Stockton. As soon as she walked through the door the Lord told me that she was my sister, even though I could instantly see the resemblance; she was very tall, like me.

As we chatted, we realised how many links there were between us already. Our dad had spent a lot of time in the area where I grew up. Tracy had known about me for years, but had been warned, even by some of the local hard men, to keep away from me because I was an absolute head-banger and was dangerous. For a while after I'd become a Christian, she had actually worked in the post office near my bench; I think she had been told about me by the staff in the post office. I'd gone in there many times and never met her.

But what also became clear is that our dad had done the same thing to her and her mum as he did to my family – left them and gone off with someone else. Tracy said she believed we had twin half-brothers by a relationship our dad had had with yet another woman. My dad hadn't wanted anything to do with them either. I don't know the full details, but it helped answer some difficult questions for me. There were so many times as a child that I thought Dad had left because of something I'd done, even though I was only a baby at the time. Looking back now, what caused him to leave was obviously his lack of commitment, his inability to deal with responsibility and his drink problem – not me. I had a lot of deep emotional wounds, but finding out information like this has helped to heal me.

Tracy also told me why everyone was so shocked to see me at the funeral. At the beginning of the service, I had crept in at the back of the church and then tried to slip out again when the service was over. But just as I was trying to leave, everyone suddenly turned around to go too. They all stopped and stared at me in horror – I can still remember the looks on their faces. Apparently, I am the spitting image of my dad, so it was a shock for everyone to see this figure at the back of the church who looked just like the man in the coffin – almost as if a ghost was watching his own funeral!

But one of the biggest shocks was finding out about the murder of my dad's mum – and who the killer was. Apparently, around the time I was born, dad's mum had been killed in what was considered to be a crime of passion. What was stranger still is that I know the man who did it. He served time for manslaughter and has now become a Christian. My sister brought me newspaper clippings of the murder trial that her mum had given her. My dad had apparently kept them for years. I would never tell this man that it was my dad's mum that he killed, because I wouldn't want him to ever think that I held anything against him – I never knew her or my dad and I'm 100 per cent certain this man has paid for his crime. Maybe one day he will learn about the link between us – but I believe it has to be in the Lord's timing.

Tracy and I got to know each other more, and she came to one of my talks. She wants to come to more of them in the future. It feels nice to know I've got a sister, and I hope we'll stay in touch. It might help to piece together more of the puzzle of my past.

However, despite having to work through issues and frequently talk about my old life, my main focus has to be on the future and the vision the Lord has given for the work of Sowing Seeds Ministries. We support people of all ages, but mainly children and teenagers, either in prison or at risk of going to prison. I think the charity will focus even more exclusively on them over the next couple of years, as we develop certain projects. One project is Bad Boys Born Again. The idea is that a gang of tough lads will visit various places to talk about how their lives have been changed by the Lord and how there is a better way to live. Kids will be given good role models and will see that Christianity is not for wimps, but for strong people who have the courage to be different.

Another project we are planning to set up is called The Father's Heart. We want to offer schools a consistent programme over a number of weeks, tailored to their needs. The programme will include teaching on things such as citizenship and drug and alcohol awareness, offered through mentoring, RE classes and residential events. We had an away weekend with some kids to pilot the idea and it was a great success.

I've also recently set up a discipleship group for new Christians or for those showing an interest in the Lord. We meet on a Tuesday afternoon at Power League, play football or pool, chat, pray, have Bible studies and deal with any issues lads need to talk about; it's encouraging for them to have that support as they grow in their faith. Between five and eleven lads meet, and some in the group have become Christians. New Christians have brought non-Christian friends along and I think the group will continue to grow and develop.

We have big plans for the future. The idea for one came from Patrick Hinton. He visited a self-run Christian community in Barcelona, part of Remar International. The chief executive is an ex lifer who wanted to create a community in which people would support each other by using their particular skills – for instance, a painter would do some decorating for a baker, and the baker would pay him by making him a cake. They live off the land and have their own animals. And they live by faith – often they will pray for provision and someone will turn up unexpectedly with exactly what they need.

Something has always really excited me about this idea. I believe the Lord wants us to run a complex in a similar way, including a farm, a church, a café, tent missions and an assault course. Excluded kids could come and undergo training and gain qualifications, to give themselves a better future. It could also be open to the surrounding community, there would perhaps be a park and restaurant they could use, but mainly it would be for excluded kids or those just released from prison who have nowhere to go.

The Lord has also shown me some of the trouble we might have, but we have to look at the bigger picture and all the positive outcomes Jesus can bring about.

I have also had another vision – something we would like to call Caleb's Place. While I was at my mam's in Portugal, the Lord gave me a picture of a cross-shaped complex in which we could provide different types of help for ex offenders. It would help them get back into society, and would have swimming facilities and a therapeutic area for lads damaged and ill from drug and alcohol abuse.

We want to call it Caleb's Place not because Caleb is my son's name. It's because of a man called Caleb in the Bible. He showed great faith and encouraged people (see Numbers chapter 13, verses 17–30). In the story, Moses, the man leading the nation of Israel at that time, sent a group of men to spy on the land the Lord had promised to give them to live in. When the spies returned from their mission, most of them reported the difficulties to be faced if Israel tried to take the land – the people living there were like giants, and they thought they couldn't overcome them. But, Caleb stood up and declared that Israel should go and take the land because they were more than able to do it. He had faith in God's promise. This is the message of Caleb's Place. A lot of these kids have been told for so many years that they can't overcome their problems and achieve, but we believe the Lord wants them to know that they can do it; they can have successful lives.

We also have an idea to set up a Christian nightclub on a Friday night, with some really good Christian music and no alcohol and drugs allowed. We also sense that we should set up some kind of church in a place in Middlesbrough called Captain Cook Square. Every time we go there we meet someone who we tell about Jesus and we pray for that person.

These are big visions that I believe the Lord has shown me over a number of years. However, even though I've gone through a long training period and dug deep foundations, I have to keep praying and testing these things. Sowing Seeds need a lot of funding to do all this, and the Lord told me that He would give us £1,000 a week as our foundation. I think one day we will have 1,000 people giving £1 a week in order to achieve this.

It's sometimes hard to believe these things will happen – there are some who doubt they ever will. But, I just have to look back at what the Lord has done already, exactly as He promised. Once, I remember, He gave me a picture of my past to encourage me.

It was very early one morning, Christmas 2006, when I was praying about what I believed the Lord was telling me to do. Christmas had always been very special to me as a child. I would feel happy, because my family would be together and wouldn't argue. But in the years that followed, Christmas became an excuse for drinking, and ended up being a time of sorrow. I eventually found myself alone on the streets, watching everyone else celebrate with their families. The worst Christmas Day ever was when I was too ill to walk but I had to crawl the half mile to the off licence. Since becoming a Christian, Christmas has felt almost magical again; I'm overwhelmed with joy at the significance of the Lord sending the baby Jesus into the world.

But on that particular morning in 2006, I was troubled. I was praying about leaving the employment of the church and setting up an independent charity. I didn't want to struggle financially. We'd only been in our new house for about three weeks; what if we couldn't afford to keep it? What would happen to my family?

As I was pondering all this, I looked out of the dark window and saw my reflection. Then, in the presence of the Lord, I also saw standing beside me Natasha, her sister Naomi and my brother-in-law Ike, before he married Naomi. It was a picture of when I first met them all in 1998. As I continued to look, I saw behind them two other people. They became clearer, and I saw that they were my sons, Caleb and Boaz. The Lord said to me, 'Can you see what I knew then?'

Sowing Seeds was about to be birthed the following year, but I didn't know it. The Lord was increasing my faith, belief and hope in His plans for the future, using a picture from my past and giving me the assurance that He is always with me and always will be – to the end of the age (see Matthew chapter 28, verse 20).

The hope I now have in my life is not just for Christmas. The festive season is still my favourite time of the year, but knowing Jesus means that every day feels like Christmas. Life can be hard work – upsetting, painful, confusing – but knowing how much the Lord loves me brings me great joy.

M LEFT:
h Howard, Police Sergeant Brian McCarthy and
at a Christian Police Association presentation.
vas at Keith's church that I — ex con Gram —
ptised policeman Brian!

sockfield Secure Training Centre —
e team and I visit every Wednesday

Castington Young Offenders Institution
— another place the team visit

At one time I was behind bars; now I'm
trusted with the keys to many prisons

Mark Owens discovered that God is there for us no matter how hard things get

Ben Falaja, a boxer sponsored by Sowing Seeds Ministries

Holme House – the first prison I visited to minister, on 26 November 1998

Me and Suggs, Manchester, 18 December 2008. I never would have dreamed that Madness, my favourite band, would read my story

Me with kids from Kings Academy at Knocks Retreat Centre

THE CHAMPIONS OF 5-A-SIDE

he team at Powerleague tockton, where Sowing Seeds holds a discipleship course

n Williamson and me baptising Chris Crossan in the River Swale, Richmond, North Yorkshire, 19 April 2009

FROM LEFT:
Caleb, Natasha, me and Boaz
at our home, 4 June 2009

Under nines football team sponsored
by Sowing Seeds Ministries. My son
Caleb is on the left, wearing green

Wesland School, where the team and I take
lessons on such things as citizenship and drug
and alcohol awareness

I've found that anything is possible with the Lord – a tramp on a bench can become chief executive of a charity!

But I need other people to help me. I've got a brilliant team who want to see love in action. It's what drives us all. It has motivated me to do what I've done for the past twelve years, ever since the Lord first told me that He loves me. I've wanted to tell everyone about His love – around town, in prison, on planes, on trains, in pubs, in the bus queue, in the takeaway shop, in the leisure centre, in shops and even when I go on holiday. It's in my blood. I never want a day off – and I probably never will!

PART TWO:
MOVING TOGETHER

CHAPTER EIGHT

MEET THE TEAM

The Sowing Seeds team members share how they came to faith and came together to demonstrate love in action.

THE FATHER'S HEART

By Ian Williamson

I stared in horror at the huge drunk towering over me on the bus, offering me one of his many cans. I was eighteen and scared. Hard to imagine that years later we'd be working together, taking the love of God to lads without hope or direction; lads living the life that I once lived.

At the time of that first encounter with Gram, my life had already started spiralling downwards. I was just seven years old when it all started. Before then I'd had a good upbringing in a lovely house in the country, but it all changed when my parents divorced. My mum had no money and we had to move to a rough council estate in Middlesbrough. I didn't fit in and was bullied up until the age of sixteen. It was tough and I moved schools a lot. The bullying continued and finally came to a head when, in my final year at school, a lad tried to fight me. I didn't want to fight, but I was surrounded by kids laughing and goading me. As I backed up against a wall, I felt a loose brick behind me. I grabbed it and the lad who wanted to beat me up suddenly looked scared. Everyone stopped laughing and I ran at them with the brick in my hand. I made a decision that day: I wasn't going to be a victim any more.

By the time I started college, I'd re-invented myself as a fighter and a ladies' man – no one knew me, so I could take on this new identity. I had been the fat kid at school and not very attractive to girls, but now I had grown tall and had muscles where before there was fat. I was quite intelligent but tried to get away with doing the minimum required. Deep down I was frightened of failing – messing around and not succeeding was better than trying and not succeeding. I was throwing things away before people could take them from me.

The problem was that I had created the image of being someone I wasn't. I started taking all kinds of drugs, drinking and clubbing, because it made me feel that I was really the person I was pretending to be. It made me feel invincible and masked all my insecurities. When I was sober, I knew who I really was – someone full of fear and with no self-esteem.

By then, I was in contact with my dad, who worked offshore. He used to come home and flash thousands of pounds at me, which I would spend on clothes. He got me a job with his company and I was earning £180 a day at nineteen. I spent it on living the fast life; I thought it would finally make me happy, but the pain and fear from childhood was always there. I thought an education would make a difference, but after a year at university I left. Even though I got good marks I decided to quit while I was ahead instead of taking a risk and failing later.

My next job was managing a pub. This wasn't too bad to start with because I had met and moved in with a girl who was very sensible. She wanted to join the police and I really did care for her. I stopped taking drugs and just drank socially with my girlfriend. We were going to get married, but I was full of insecurity and was accusing her of having affairs – I was convinced she was going to leave me. Ten days before the wedding, I ended it in an appalling way, by getting drunk and shouting loads of abuse. Mind you, the way I was back then, it was the best thing that could have happened to her!

But she was the rock in my life, and then she was gone. I went off the rails – staying up all night, having lock-ins in the pub, seeing different girlfriends and gambling. The gambling and drug taking became so bad that in three years I accumulated debts of nearly £40,000.

One day I lost it completely and fled with the pub takings, my dog and a passport. I was going to go to Amsterdam, spend the money, come back and face the music. The only reason I didn't go was because the taxi driver informed me that I wouldn't be able to get in his taxi or on the plane with my dog. So there I was, wandering around the streets with my dog, £8,000 in notes and £500 in coins stuffed in my pockets.

I ended up knocking on one of the barmaid's doors at 3am, and woke up on her floor the next morning.

I returned to the pub with the money, minus a few hundred pounds. My boss was fuming, but he understood the problems I was going through. I didn't manage the bar again, but he got me a job with his brother-in-law's security firm in London. I started manning security barriers at concerts and building stages. It was my fresh start – a bit like Gram's grand plan to make a fresh start when he was released from prison! It wasn't long before I realised how expensive cocaine was in London compared to Middlesbrough. This was how I was going to make money, I thought. I got it sent down from Middlesbrough so that I could sell it and pay off my debts, but I ended up taking it myself and owing even more money. London can be a bad place when you are sensible, but when you're an idiot it's a dangerous place to be. A few people told me to get back home or I would end up in the Thames. I was very small fry even in Middlesbrough; in London I was nothing.

I went back to Teesside and started working on the doors. Every time I tried to find a way out of my problems I ended up creating more problems. I used cocaine to get rid of the fear of the job, but it made me paranoid and aggressive, so I attacked everyone. Then I got scared of revenge attacks, took even more cocaine to get rid of that fear and ended up attacking more people. It was a vicious circle of violence, drugs and failed relationships; I'd split up with another girlfriend I'd shared a house with and moved back in with my mum.

But everything came to a head one night when I threatened to kill myself in front of my family – it was during an argument about a takeaway! Mum had made my tea, but I'd brought home pizza instead. The disagreement about it was the straw that broke the camel's back. I picked up a big kitchen knife and threatened to stab myself; I'd had enough and I wanted to die. I blurted out everything about the debt, the drugs and the lifestyle I was living. My mum stopped being angry and stared at me in horror; my stepdad was sitting on the settee with his dinner on a tray, and next to him was my brother – they were both watching the scene in total disbelief. I threw the knife down, ran upstairs and cried on my bed like a baby.

Mum came up to see me. She'd had it tough for many years – raising two boys on her own and being abused by various boyfriends. But she built up her life from nothing, put herself through nursing training and had become a sister in a doctor's surgery. She had a lovely house and was married to a really nice man who didn't swear, drink, smoke or fight. I thought he was a wimp for being like that and didn't respect him. But it's funny that everything I'd despised about men who had hurt me in my life, I had become, yet this man was everything I'd wanted in a father, but I was angry at him for being that way.

My mum had become a Christian when I was about fifteen. As she sat with me in my room, she started telling me how God had changed her life and how He could change mine.

'What's He going to do, write me a ———— cheque for £40,000?' I shouted. I felt angry, like she was somehow trivialising everything that was going on in my life and she was some kind of nutter for believing in God! In the end, she took out a huge loan to cover my debts, so Jesus did help me after all, through her.

I was still working the doors and using drugs. I had to get out; I was adding to my debt instead of decreasing it. I looked around at the people running the town and they were nasty, evil men. I could be as nasty as the next man and thought somehow it was survival of the fittest. But deep down I didn't want to be that. I wanted to love and be loved. I was confused, though – I thought that to be a man you had to be aggressive and that love was somehow weak. One night in bed, I cried out for an answer. 'God, if You're there, I need to know. But I want something real – I don't want a butterfly, a rainbow or a verse out of the Bible.' I fell asleep weeping. The next morning when I woke up I felt a love and peace I'd never felt before – it was amazing. I was twenty-eight years old and it was the first time I'd woken up since I was seven without fear in my heart. I realised that my dad had been my rock and my protection and since he had left I had been wracked with fear. But I wasn't afraid any more. All my problems that had seemed like a massive mountain the day before, suddenly seemed like little molehills that could be tackled one at a time. The world seemed bright and awesome, and for the next three days I was high as a kite.

I wanted to go into psychiatric nursing and needed some voluntary experience. I approached a Christian charity, Spurgeon's Childcare, and, after speaking to the manager, was offered a full-time job. I needed to pay back my mum for the loan – you can get away with letting the banks wait, but not your mum! The job paid £16,000 a year, but Spurgeon's had made a mistake on my contract and instead paid me £19,000. It was legally binding and I was allowed to keep it at that, even though I wouldn't be allowed pay rises for a while.

The work was in the rough areas I thought I'd escaped from, helping lads like me that had no dads around and needed direction. It was a hard learning process and helped to develop me for what I'm doing now.

It was at the charity that I got to know Rachel. She worked in a different department and we realised we'd met before, but we weren't too sure where. We eventually worked it out; she used to work with my ex fiancée, and stayed over at the pub one night after going out for a drink. I'd met her in the kitchen the next morning.

'You must be Ian,' she said.

'Who else would it be?' I muttered arrogantly and walked out, munching a bowl of cornflakes.

Not a very good first impression – and I didn't do too well on our first date either! Once I realised we shared the same faith, after seeing her at a local Christian concert, I asked her out. But even though I'd had the reputation of being a bit of a gigolo, as a Christian on a date I was clueless. I had no idea how I was supposed to say goodbye, so I patted her on the head and said, 'See you later.' She must have thought I was treating her like a dog! Fortunately, she wanted to see me again – and didn't tell anyone at work what I used to be like, which was something I was worried about.

But as a Christian, I was struggling. I was secretly battling with my drug habit, and the church I went to had an elderly congregation I couldn't relate to. I felt part of two worlds: my church world and the real world. I was lonely and knew very few Christians apart from the old people I met once a week on a Sunday. I was almost at the point of a nervous breakdown.

I decided to talk to Brian and Cilla Jones. They are a lovely couple, with a big country house that they invite drug addicts and the homeless into for meals and barbecues. I had met them once the year before, but when I knocked on their door with Rachel at 10.30pm, they opened the door and said, 'Hi Ian,' as if I were their best friend – they had remembered me from that one meeting a year ago. They showed me the love of Christ, helped me find a flat and started discipling me morning, noon and night. I needed it. I'd lived in both camps for too long and I knew both the reality of God and the sin I was in.

Meanwhile, my relationship with Rachel was quite turbulent. She has a child from a previous marriage, Hannah, and she had a lot of baggage and fear as a result of that relationship. I had all my baggage too, so we needed a lot of counselling. We were advised to wait before we considered marriage. But I wasn't one to listen to authority and told Rachel that we needed to marry or split up so that it didn't confuse Hannah. We had a difficult couple of years after marrying, with a lot to work through, but God helped us. We've knocked the edges off each other, so we can see the reasons for the struggles now. We've also suffered three miscarriages, but our daughter Esther Hope was born in 2008 – named so because we never gave up hope.

My brother has seen the change in me and has told me he's proud of me. We have a great relationship now, but I wasn't very nice to him as a child, which is something I really regret. I was convinced he was Mum's favourite and used to physically and mentally abuse him. I took out a lot of my anger on him and wanted him to feel as bad as I did. He's also had a lot of problems with drugs, but from seeing me as a quitter, he knows I'm sticking at things now. He used to think Rachel and I couldn't be Christians because we were always arguing, but now he believes there must be a God because of the changes in me – I've been clean for three years now and Rachel and I don't drink. He's asked me to pray for him.

God has also brought healing in other areas. Not only did He take away the anger and rejection I felt towards my dad for leaving, but also He replaced it with love and a new understanding of my dad and the problems he faced in his own childhood. He was only nineteen when he married – just a kid really – and his experience of marriage and family life was far from ideal. He came from a large family brought up in Park End, a tough Middlesbrough estate. Money was very tight and my mum told me stories of my dad being made to wear sandals in winter and wellies in summer because they were cheaper out of season. School wasn't much better, and his introduction to Jesus was from nuns brandishing the cane. Life was very hard – and so was his dad. Standing at over 6ft tall and weighing around nineteen stone, granddad was an angry Glaswegian who showed little affection and a lot of discipline. My dad was never shown the Father's heart, but often experienced his father's wrath and had to witness a lot of aggression and violence.

So, I could fully understand why my dad made mistakes, but also that he too needed healing from his past. I'm not sure he can accept my forgiveness, but I want him to understand just how much I love and forgive him.

But the pattern went back another generation. My granddad had little love shown to him by his own dad, my great grandfather. He was a bare-knuckle boxer and ran a gym in Glasgow. But all too often he brought his work home with him, and my granddad, his siblings and mother often suffered at the hands of this angry man. It was so bad that my granddad lied about his age to join the Navy. He was just fourteen, and chose to be torpedoed by the Germans rather than stay at home and suffer at the hands of his dad.

Four angry men, from generation to generation, all needing to see the Father's heart, all struggling with anger and self-destruction and passing that behaviour on to their children. It is only now, through God, that this cycle has been broken and God has given me and my family a second chance. It's His example I now follow. I am far from perfect and I make plenty of mistakes, but day by day, by getting closer to Jesus, I become a better father, husband and son.

Although I had a new direction and a new example to follow, it took many years for God to transform me. The angry and violent feelings that have been passed down through several generations were still there at first and it was at that point that Gram came back into my life. One day I was angry about something and wanted to sort out things in my usual way, through violence. I phoned an ex girlfriend and told her that I was a Christian and needed to find a good church. She wasn't a Christian, but had heard of the Oakwood Centre, in Eaglescliffe, so she took me there one evening. I thought I would stand out like a sore thumb as a skinhead wearing a leather jacket, but when I walked in I realised that half the people in there looked like me!

Then a giant stood up and started talking about his own anger issues and how God had dealt with them and I suddenly realised that it was the drunk from the bus all those years ago. This was a far cry from our first meeting! I had got onto an empty bus at Middlesbrough station and he suddenly appeared with two carrier bags full of lager.

You just know when the idiot's going to come and sit next to you, even when there's a load of empty seats – and he did. He leaned over and showed me what was left of his finger, which had just been chopped off, telling me all about it and the rest of his war wounds! He offered me a can, talked about football violence, asked who I knew in the town and wanted to know where I was going. I just kept thinking: please leave me alone! I was quite intimidated as an eighteen-year-old, and I'd never fought anyone as big as him. I kept hoping he'd get off at the next stop, but he got off at the one after me. I couldn't believe it.

And here he was, giving a talk about God! I went straight up to him afterwards.

'Have you got your little finger missing?'

'Yes,' he said. 'Why do you ask?' He vaguely remembered the incident I told him about.

By now I was working for the King's Academy School as a learning mentor. I was frustrated because I thought I could be doing more to help these kids, but couldn't at the time. I had some big ideas for a farm complex where kids could have training and gain qualifications. The principal thought they were good ideas, but more suitable for an individual project, not for the school.

'I think you might be in the wrong role,' he told me. 'I don't want to lose you but don't want to keep you boxed in either.'

About this time a Christian teacher gave me a prophecy, which was: 'It's time for you to move on, but you are not ready to carry the mantle yet. You need to come under an Elijah, someone like Gram or Martin Ruddick.'

Mine and Gram's paths continued to cross and one day I shared my vision with him about the farm and training and he was really excited about it – it confirmed what the Lord had said to him.

'I think you're an answer to prayer, but I don't know which one,' he said. 'God has told me that you are going to work for the charity and he is going to provide the money.'

'That's good enough for me,' I said, and handed in my notice!

It wasn't until the month before I was due to leave my job at the school that the funds came through for my salary. I told Rachel about the new opportunity.

'You will have to hand your notice in at work,' she said.

'I've already done that, pet!'

People I knew couldn't decide whether I'd acted in great faith or great stupidity. I knew it was the right thing to do and I wasn't throwing something away that was precious to me, as I was ready to move on anyway. The real step of faith came from my wife. She was working in social services and was earning good money and had her independence, but she believed God was telling her to give it up in order to support what I was doing. On paper, we looked as though we were so much worse off but, in reality, we've not wanted for anything and Rachel's been able to support me and enjoy her children more; she often used to be tired and stressed from work, but she's much freer now and a lot happier. That's worth more than anything.

As part of Sowing Seeds, I go into Kirklevington Grange, Holme House, Castington and some schools and community venues. We also have the new projects Bad Boys Born Again and The Father's Heart. Through these particularly we want to show lads at risk of getting into trouble what being a man is really all about. Their only role models are criminals and addicts, but through the fatherly love I have for these kids, I want them to understand about true strength in God and the best role model in Jesus.

The work is often hard and sometimes I think these people

don't deserve help. It is then that God reminds me that I used to be like that. I'm appalled by some of the crimes, but through God I now see the reality – they are just frightened little boys like I used to be, and but for the grace of God I could have been in the same position. I just want to show them the same love that Jesus showed me. I feel like I've got the cure for cancer and I know that everyone wants that cure deep down. But even if just a few lads can experience what I now have, it's worth all the hard work. It's disheartening when lads fail, but I have to look at how many times I've failed and remember the Christians who persevered with me. It's not just a job; it's a privilege to be doing what I'm doing.

ALL IN GOD'S TIME
By Nina Dennis

There are times when I want to pinch myself because I think I'm dreaming! As administrator for Sowing Seeds, I believe I've got a job in a million and I still can't believe God chose me for this role. But up until I joined the team, I believe God put me through a long period of preparation – sometimes painful, confusing and frightening – in order to be where I am now.

I became a Christian at the age of thirty-five at a church that some friends told me about. I'd heard that the services started at 6pm and they were still throwing people out at 10.30pm. I was sceptical but curious, so decided to go and have a look. However, even though Sundays were normally quiet, they suddenly became really busy with lots of activity and visitors. Eventually, after a couple of months, everything settled down and I grabbed the opportunity. When I arrived, the church was packed and there was an American standing at the front preaching fire and brimstone. But the presence of the Lord in that room was just overwhelming. I couldn't wait to get back the next week, when I accepted the invitation to give my life to the Lord.

Up until then I had believed I was a Christian. I had been brought up in the Church of England and attended Sunday services, but even though I felt God's presence and came out determined to be a good person for the week, it only lasted until Wednesday! But throughout my childhood nobody had ever told me that Jesus loved me. I'd always felt an emptiness; I knew there was more to life, but I didn't know what that 'more' was. But as a Christian I had a new peace and knowledge that we're not just like rabbits – born to eventually die. That sense of being loved and valued made me feel complete. I think the longing to be loved came from being from a Yorkshire family who didn't know how to show love (some of us Yorkshire people are well known for our 'no nonsense' attitude).

As a new Christian I also had revelations that my family belonged to God and that the miracles of the Bible really had taken place – I had always thought the 5,000 must have been fed because they'd all brought packed lunches!

After about six months my husband, Keith, noticed the change in me. We had some heated discussions about our beliefs, especially when we talked about the devil. He got so angry and said it was rubbish. But God was changing him too – a week later he was reading a newspaper report about Peter Sutcliffe, the killer known as 'the Yorkshire Ripper'.

'It's not hard to tell who's behind this,' he told me.

'What do you mean?'

'Why, it's the devil of course!'

But I had no idea what I was about to face. One night, in June 1997, I attended a prayer meeting and the leader said he believed he had a word from God for me. He put his hand on my head and said, 'If you are willing, I, the Lord, will be glorified in your life, but I require you to cease being a wife, cease being a mother and to cease working for the family business.'

'Lord, how can I not be a wife?' I asked, confused. But I knew I had to say yes, not really understanding what would be required.

Several hours later, at 2am, my husband died of a brain haemorrhage. He was only forty-five. It hit our family incredibly hard. I'd known him since I was thirteen and we were best friends. We'd been married for twenty-three years at that point and our sons were fourteen and eighteen.

Later, a lot of people said to me that he had told everyone he believed what I believed. But it was when I cried out to the Lord on the night Keith died that the Lord comforted me with the words: 'Don't worry – Keith is with me and is My friend.'

If it wasn't for the fact that I needed to earn money, I would have become a recluse. We had a plumbing and heating business and I kept it going. We were members of the Association of Plumbing and Heating Contractors and I kept up the membership and eventually became president of Teesside Association and then the North East Association. I was asked to consider putting myself forward for national president, but I declined. Up until this period I had no ambition and was happy to be the little wife in the background, very shy and quiet, but suddenly I had to run a business and make decisions and speeches as president. I believe this was God moulding me in preparation for my future role.

After a number of years I felt the Lord telling me it was time to step down from my role in the business, which I handed over to my son. So, that was two out of the three things the Lord had wanted me to stop. The third one, ceasing to be a mother, came about when my sons got married. I was still their mum, of course, and we are very close, but the relationships changed; I no longer had that sole responsibility for them on a day-to-day basis. One had married a few years previously but the other married on 16 June 2007 – almost ten years to the day since God had first given me the prophecy, on 19 June 1997.

Just three months later, I joined Sowing Seeds. After giving up the business, I still needed to work, but every time I went to the jobcentre, it felt as though the Lord was putting His hand up and saying 'No'. It was then that I was sent an email about Sowing Seeds needing an administrator.

I'd often heard about this 'big Gram', but I was always away when he came to our church to give talks. When he phoned me, we hit it off straight away and I knew that even if I didn't get the job, I really wanted to be involved in the work.

I feel so blessed in this role, but sometimes it's painful when you see some of the kids that the team are helping. Some of the letters are heartbreaking and there have been many times when we've sat in the office and cried. Here are kids with no self-worth, pouring out their hearts to you in a letter – some of them can't be that open face to face. But we know the only one who can really help them is Jesus.

When God touches their lives, it's such a blessing to us. When Gram rings up and tells me about things that have happened, I feel breathless because it's so awesome. It's such a privilege to be involved in this amazing ministry.

GAME OF LIFE

By Eric Young

To me it was passion and excitement; a snapshot of life thrown at you, with all its highs and lows, concentrated into ninety minutes of play. Like life, there were no second chances. But also like life, it meant everything and I was lost without it. It was only when I found something to fill the gap that I was able to live again.

Football has been my passion since childhood. By the time I was a teenager I had played for England Schoolboys and had all the top clubs wanting to sign me as an apprentice – in fact, former players Jackie Milburn and Len Shackleton described me in the press as 'the finest young player they had ever seen from the North East', which was some compliment. Having a father from Manchester, I supported Manchester United, and at fifteen years old I had the opportunity to live the dream – I turned my back on school and moved to Manchester to join United.

I almost broke into the first team and had some exciting moments. My idol was Denis Law, so training with him was like a dream come true; in fact, he used to pick me up in his car to take me to training and I would sit there, saying nothing, just pinching myself! I could never get over the fact I was a United player, but deep down I could never accept that a kid from a council estate in Stockton could ever play for them and would often freeze when an opportunity came my way. I had a bit of the 'Groucho Marks syndrome' – why would I want to join a club that would have someone like me as a member!

I also loved the challenge, the excitement and the camaraderie in the dressing room; the opportunity to be creative, the laughs, the characters and brotherhood that develops amongst the team and also the honesty – if you weren't doing your stuff they would soon let you know.

Even though I played as a professional with the England Youth team when I was eighteen, my overall progress was hindered by the transition the club was going through with the change of managers after Sir Matt Busby. I was on loan to Peterborough United when the manager Frank O'Farrell at United was sacked and Tommy Docherty took over. O'Farrell had assured me I was one of the players that he would not let go, and wanted to build a new team around me and Sammy McIlroy, but the new manager brought in his own players. This is how fortunes change in football, and when I returned to the club I asked for a transfer. I ended up having spells with Walsall and Stockport County, before returning to the North East to join Darlington.

But as my football career was taking off, I suffered personal tragedy. Unknown to me, my sister, Dawn, had had a kidney removed when she was eleven and her life expectancy wasn't good. She died when she was just twenty-three. A year after that I was back at the same grave burying my father, who was only forty-seven. The graveside experience had a profound effect on me and I believe something died in me that day. I also suffered from chronic homesickness. Football no longer had the same importance and I began to question the meaning of life. I had always considered myself to be a believer, but had been brought up as a Roman Catholic and attending church was a chore I undertook so that I didn't risk losing my salvation.

Ten years after entering professional football, I left to get married. I no longer wanted to scrape a living in the lower leagues, so sought more security in a sales job and played football part time. Although better off financially,

I soon realised I had left prematurely and suffered what I can only describe as an inner panic; there was no substitute for the game.

So when an opportunity came to go to Australia in 1980, as a player/coach for a Tasmanian team, I leapt at the chance. I had to find a day job to supplement the role, but I was so successful on the field that I was in demand to go to other parts of Australia. After a spell in Victoria and Western Australia, my wife fell pregnant. She had followed me around Australia but was homesick and wanted to be near her family. We returned to the UK and I joined the police force in 1985.

I couldn't adjust to life after leaving professional football and felt lost. I often worked the beat on a Saturday, patrolling the streets when I should have been at a match. Even now, after all these years, Fridays still have a special place in my life – I'm still mentally preparing my mind for the next day's game.

I became very depressed and on many days dreaded going into work. I loved becoming a father, though, and persevered with the police to provide for my family, but hoped that one day we would return to Australia.

I had stopped going to church by this time, but when I joined the police, I and the others starting with me were given a Bible by The Gideons Society. I remember them telling us not to throw it away because one day we might be glad of it. Those words came true at one of my lowest points.

After six years of marriage, my wife announced that she was leaving and moved to London with our twenty-month-old daughter. I was devastated and my world fell apart. I couldn't understand it and blamed myself for not being happy because of my work. But, in addition, after losing my father and sister, it felt as though I was losing a family for the second time. It became too much to bear.

I wasn't told where my wife and daughter were, and we

had no contact for six months. Eventually I began to get some contact with my daughter, but it was like borrowing a library book for a few hours that then had to be returned. I had to be satisfied with a few hours' contact once a month, travelling to London each time. This continued for about three years and was distressing and humiliating. I felt as though someone had reached into my chest, grabbed my heart, pulled it out and then tossed it away. What compounded this was that 'the system' refused to acknowledge the trauma a father goes through in these situations; they only seemed concerned about how much money they could extract.

I felt I had lost everything. This was in the days before Fathers for Justice, when dads dressed as Batman and Robin climbed onto Buckingham Palace or motorway bridges to protest against the injustice of being prevented from seeing their children. In my mind I wanted to do the same and shout about it from the top of Nelson's Column. Instead, I wrote to the press, joined a father's support group and was featured on the BBC's *Everyman* documentary about fathers and divorce. It's something I have always felt strongly about and I believe there's a huge need to reinstate the importance of fathers in families, if only for the sake of our young men who need masculine input and discipline. I believe the needs of the family should come before the needs of the individual, just as the team is bigger than the player. I think of what Jesus said: 'I and the Father are one' and yet '... the Father is greater than I' (John 10:30; 14:28).

After the *Everyman* programme, I was allowed to have my daughter at home with me for holidays, and many who saw the programme offered me the use of their home when visiting London, rather than having to wander the streets for hours. It helped to restore my faith in human nature.

My daughter has now grown into a fine young woman,

building her own life, but while I was trying to cope with all this, I felt empty inside. One evening I noticed the Gideons Bible on my bedside cabinet. I reached for it, saying: 'Go on then, hit me – give me Your best shot. Let's see what You are made of!'

I had rarely seen a Bible before. I had been taught as a Catholic that the Church had to interpret the Bible for us in case we misinterpreted it ourselves. I had thumbed through one occasionally, but found it difficult to understand. However, reading through the Gospels that evening it all suddenly became very real for the first time. It was as though Jesus was speaking directly to me, into my life, and I knew no mere man could have spoken with such depth and wisdom. I was knocking at the door and it was being opened, but this time I was doing it with all my heart. I couldn't put it down. Everything I'd previously been taught about God was brushed aside and I began to slowly re-educate myself through reading the Word, building up a new understanding and faith. For the first time since finishing football I found something I could get excited and passionate about.

I became involved in Sportsreach, a Christian ministry that runs soccer schools, takes teams abroad and shares the gospel through sport. I travelled with them to many countries and was also given the opportunity to fulfil a dream of mine. Since discovering the Bible, I had a longing to study it in more depth at Bible college, but thought that this was just for church ministers and I had no desire to be one. I had also been haunted by the fact that I'd given up on my education as a teenager. But through Sportsreach I took a year-long career break from the police and attended Capernwray Hall Bible School in Carnforth, North Lancashire. I completed the spring and winter courses with distinction and loved every second of it.

I work with a lot of troubled lads, but it seems that God is using the Father's heart in me, which had no outlet, for the benefit of these boys – a lost generation of young men who need male role models in their lives and adventurous activities to get them off the streets. I could see they needed a controlled environment to burn off their testosterone in manly pursuits, and challenge and competition to stretch them to their full capabilities. Sport was an excellent way for me to help them do that.

I had been introduced to Gram through a mutual friend in the police, Brian McCarthy, and we were talking about this over coffee one day. I had retired from the force by then and Gram asked if I would assist with some of the young offenders at Hassockfield. I joined the team and now run four eight-week football courses a year. It's proved a really excellent way of teaching the lads on the football field, rather than them being lectured at in the classroom; principles such as the value of teamwork, the need for rules, practice, perseverance and how to deal with both success and failure. I also talk to them about what it is to be a man, accepting responsibility and having self-discipline not simply brute force. I explain the similarities in living the Christian life.

We have also started working in some of the schools that deal with the excluded children and have taken a group of boys for an adventure weekend in the Lakes, which proved a success. It's a privilege to be involved with Gram and Sowing Seeds. Football is still in my blood, and my heart always leaps when I see a football pitch! But I can only think that the seeds I'm now sowing in these lads' lives will one day make a difference, maybe years from now. I can see the Holy Spirit at work in their lives already, and it makes me smile. I also have the satisfaction of knowing I'm in God's will and I'm being used by Him. I have met so many brothers and sisters in Christ from around the world and although it hurts not having a family, God told me He would give me a family bigger than I could possibly imagine – and He has.

THE GOD-SHAPED GAP

By Lynn Woodwark

Another failed relationship – why did this keep happening to me?

I couldn't get enough of men – it was like an addiction. Most of them were married, which suited my needs, but it only ever satisfied me temporarily. My life was still empty – I felt like I had a big hole inside me that could never be filled. I was miserable.

I was a lapsed Catholic, but when my friend's marriage started breaking up, I decided to go to church to pray for the family – the first time I would have been in twenty years, apart from weddings and funerals. But it still took several weeks before I did actually go.

Around this time my friend's eleven-year-old son committed his life to Jesus at a Billy Graham satellite meeting, and his mother started taking him to a Baptist church. Meanwhile, I finally planned my church visit one bank holiday weekend. However, the day before, I woke up feeling really restless and I wasn't sure why. I paced up and down in my small flat, feeling like a caged animal, until I couldn't stand it any longer. I walked to a local beauty spot in the pouring rain, talking to the trees, the sky – anything that would listen. But there was nobody there. I went home to change out of my soaking clothes.

I felt so terrible I didn't even know if I could make it to work that night. For some reason, I took out a Bible and looked at the page that fell open. It was the book of Esther, chapter 2. I struggled to read it, gave up in disgust and slung the Bible under a chair – I couldn't read the English, let alone the Hebrew names.

Without warning, a couple from work turned up, so I had to focus on them for a while, and eventually made it to work, finishing at 5.30am. I set the alarm, so that I could go to church and pray for my friend, and when I got there, I discovered that it was a Baptist church – different to anything I had experienced before.

The minister suddenly started preaching on Esther 2 – the chapter I had read at random the day before! I knew something was going on, but wasn't sure what. At the end of the service I started talking to a man in the congregation, who explained what it meant to be born again. I had heard that Cliff Richard was born again, but assumed that it was another religion. When I got home I thought about what I had been told, but that was when the battle started in my mind. I was aware that if I was going to act on what I'd heard, it would cost me my sex life – and I wasn't prepared to give that up.

I struggled with this for the next week, but then realised that nothing in my life had changed for the better. I decided that if what I had been told was a load of rubbish, I wouldn't be any worse off by believing, but if it was true, there was a chance I could miss out on something. I decided to believe Jesus was the Son of God, confess my sins (which were many) and ask Jesus into my life.

Two things happened straight away: I stopped swearing, after many failed attempts to clean up my foul mouth, and the empty space inside me got filled up with God. I started going to church and enjoying it. Jesus had started to change my life. If anyone had told me even two weeks before that

I would be going to church and reading the Bible, I would have laughed in their face!

I was attending All Nations Church and heard that Sowing Seeds needed extra help in the office. I had just spent some time in hospital and was worried about finding work again, even though I had worked for the police in communications for the past twenty-three years. I thought I was too old.

I prayed about helping Sowing Seeds and said, 'Lord, if it's what You want for me, can You prompt Nina to ask me – then I will know that I am able to do the job.'

One Sunday at church, Nina approached me about the work. She later shared that she had said to the Lord that if I was the first person she saw when she arrived at church, she would know to ask me – and I was!

I'm so thankful to the Lord for His leading and so blessed to be working for Gram and being involved in everything that's happening. But more than anything, I know that hole inside me will remain filled with God – nothing else but Him can fill the gap.

LOVE IS THE KEY

By Brian Foskett

The night I looked at a dirty, drunken tramp and loved him, I knew God had given me something special. It could not have possibly come from me; He had shown me how much He loved people, and placed in me His love for them.

I'd been a Christian six months when it happened. I was helping out in the grounds of the church I attended, when my children rushed around the corner and told me there was a tramp hanging around the other side. He appeared with his carrier bags full of cider bottles and instead of telling him to go away, which others were telling him to do, I asked him to stay with me, as long as he didn't drink. He struggled a bit – looking at his bags then looking at me – but he left them alone and stayed with me for the next few hours. The Lord gave me a tremendous love for him, and I knew there was something I should tell him.

'Jesus loves you,' I said.

'He couldn't possibly love someone like me,' he responded. I told him all about Jesus and what He had done for him, and the tears were running down his face; he then gave his life to the Lord.

My own salvation at the age of forty-two took a lot longer. I was involved in Sunday school as a child, but as an adult I had little connection with church. My wife, Iris, took our four daughters to church until they were teenagers, and for eighteen years I dropped them off, went home to read the Sunday papers and picked them up again afterwards. One Saturday night in 1985, God spoke to me and told me to go to church the next morning – that shocked my family! It was the start of God drawing me near to Him. At the time I had smoked forty cigarettes a day for twenty-four years and could not stop because of my addiction, but I decided to give up for Lent, as this would be the most difficult thing for me to do for the Lord. I never smoked again.

But it wasn't until I went to my friends' church that things changed dramatically. As soon as I walked in I felt so embarrassed; there were people dancing in the aisles, waving their hands in the air and speaking in languages I didn't understand. If I could have crawled under the seat I would have done! But I knew they had something that I didn't have – they loved each other and seemed so happy. I kept going back, and on the third occasion when the preacher asked anyone who wanted to give his or her life to Jesus to come forward, I couldn't even remember getting out of my seat. I was as far away as you could possibly be from the front and suddenly I was at the front. As soon as I made that decision for Jesus to be Lord of my life, I was like the cat that had got the cream. It was absolutely amazing – a total transformation. The most important decision I have ever made in my life was on that Friday night in November 1986.

At that time I was General Manager of a large motor dealership I had worked in for twenty-three years. Being a Christian didn't go down well with some of the directors because it was a pretty cutthroat industry. I started to really love people and I felt out of place.

In November 1989, God told me I had to leave the company and it was one of the most difficult decisions I have ever had to make; I had a big mortgage, four daughters, company cars and an expense account. My wife, who attended church at the time, but did not know Jesus as her Lord, said that if that's what I was supposed to do, I should do it. She had more faith than me! I struggled with it for a couple of days, eventually handed in my notice and walked out with nothing. Within forty-eight hours a Christian friend offered me a job in financial services, which was what I did for the next eleven years. It was a lesson in faith for me, to trust the Lord. When He says do something, do it. He doesn't say, 'If you do this I will give you that.' There's not much faith in that.

In November 1991, I and two Christian friends believed that the Lord had told us to start a church in Marton. This was the farthest thing from my mind, however we knew that it was of the Lord. It began in the friends' house and I took the role of pastor whilst working full time. As the church grew, we moved to community centres and schools and ended up buying what is now All Nations Church, Hemlington, where

Sowing Seeds have their offices. I remained the pastor until January 2008 – a total of seventeen years, the last seven of which I worked for the church full time.

I had known Gram for years and he ran some Alpha courses for us at church. I asked him if he could get me into Holme House Prison in January 2008 because one of our church members was in there, and whilst I was there visiting he invited me to talk to the lads. It felt so natural and I felt a tremendous love for them. I had worked in prisons before – years ago I visited lads in Deerbolt when I was part of the Full Gospel Business Men's Fellowship. I've always felt as though God has given me His heart and eyes in order to love them.

I volunteered for the charity at first, and was later invited to become a part-time staff member. One of my roles is to promote the charity among churches and hopefully find churches and individuals who will partner with us in prayer and financially, as well as volunteering to work within our ministry. I agreed to this on the condition that I could still work with the lads in prison. I wanted to be on the frontline and to be able to talk about the work first hand. So, as well as promotional work, I visit Holme House three times a week, Kirklevington Grange once a week, Full Sutton regularly, support lads in court and meet them on release and help find them churches and homes if they want me to.

It's been fantastic to see God move in the lives of these lads. In Holme House alone I had the privilege of leading twenty-four lads to the Lord during 2008. One of the most memorable recently was Chris. He was only twenty-four and had been an addict since he was nine years old; his father used to give him drugs. He had lost his childhood and his teenage years and most of his life had been a blur.

I saw him when he was on remand for theft and he gave his life to the Lord in one of the groups with which I worked.

He stopped taking drugs and drinking, stopped fighting and started asking a lot of questions. He also started telling other lads about the Lord. Once I was with him and he was talking to another lad, who suddenly said, 'I want Jesus too.' This was at 3.45pm – the time the guards always come to lock the lads up in their cells. I prayed the guards would be late for once, and for the first time ever they were – they came at 4pm!

I attended Durham Crown Court with Chris to give him moral support. As I waited in the public gallery, Chris's case kept getting put back because his barrister was in the other court. There were three other people in the gallery and I felt prompted to go and talk to two of them. I asked if they had anything to do with Chris and they turned out to be his mother and stepfather.

I told them how Chris had been totally transformed and, unknown to me, his stepfather went to find the solicitor, who asked me to write a statement to give to the barrister. As soon as Chris's case came up, God spoke to me and said, 'Don't worry about what you should say. I will fill your mouth.' I didn't understand this at the time; all the judge was going to do was hear my written statement. However, as soon as he heard it, he summoned me to the witness box and, as God had promised, the words just came out.

'Right, I've heard enough!' the judge interrupted me. When he addressed Chris he said, 'I'd already made up my mind to give you eighteen months today, but because of what Mr Foskett's told me, I'm going to give you another chance.' Chris received two years on probation. His mother was in tears. I waited for him to be released and drove them home. For the whole journey Chris was witnessing to his mum.

What can happen when lads become Christians is that they can easily be discouraged and give up when they come up against problems. We fixed Chris up with a church and someone to look after him, but it got to the point where he wouldn't answer my phone calls. We lost contact and his probation officer said she was worried about him – he'd gone right back into his shell.

I went to see him and found out he was struggling. He wanted his life right with the Lord, but he'd gone downhill, drinking and getting into fights. But this time when he was fighting, he wasn't retaliating, so he was getting hurt. I prayed with him as he put things right with God and the Holy Spirit was so powerful on him that his face was glowing. I even told him to look in the mirror because all the colour had come back.

'I was ashamed to get in touch with you, Brian. I thought you'd be really angry with me,' he told me later.

'God doesn't condemn you and neither do I. But let's get it right,' I said. We need to make sure we are there for lads like Chris as they continue with the Lord. No one can do it alone without that support.

But despite the difficulties and sometimes the disappointments involved in our ministry, I love to see the Lord work in people's lives. Because of this I always tell people that my job is fun and I want it to stay fun. I'm officially at retirement age, but you don't get to retire in God's kingdom because there's so much still to be done. Anyway, I would be bored stiff if I did retire!

RENEWED HOPE

By Mike Gallagher

The moment I knew that there was so much more to life was when a stranger spoke to me about the death of my sister.

It was something the woman couldn't possibly have known about.

I'm from a family of six children, brought up in a village fifteen miles outside Middlesbrough. My sister Frances was two years younger than me, and when she was nineteen, she was having difficulties with her boyfriend. I had been told something about him I needed to tell her. On the day I planned to tell her, she was so upset after arguing with him, that I put off speaking to her – something I would live to regret.

The next day, I told her what I needed to say. She burst into tears, rushed out of the house, drove away and was involved in a car accident. She died instantly. It was three days before my twenty-first birthday.

It was unreal – in fact, it didn't really hit home until I bought the local newspaper and sat on a bench reading it. She was such a wonderful girl and everyone loved her. In fact, all my mates used to chat her up and always asked me if I was bringing her when we went out.

I was in a daze for a long time and couldn't function properly. I blamed myself. But it was only after a woman approached my other sister in a printer's shop three months after Frances' death, that something was revealed to me.

My sister rushed home to tell me. This woman had said she knew all about Frances. I agreed to go with my sister to see her, but sat there with my arms folded, not really listening. Anyone could have picked up that information from the local media.

But then she looked at me and said, 'Frances just wants to tell you that she's OK, but you've got to stop thinking what you are thinking, because it would have been both of you.' It was unbelievable. I had told nobody up until that point that I had regretted not being in the car with Frances that night; I thought I could have somehow prevented the accident.

We never saw the woman again, but for me she confirmed that this life isn't all there is.

I went through a very low time in my life and ended up ill in hospital. I'd been brought up a Catholic and saw church as a chore I couldn't wait to get out of, but when I came out of hospital, I made a pact with God: if He could get me through this, I was going to change my life.

My mum asked me to come to church and I refused at first, but when I finally agreed, I felt a real sense of peace there and knew that something was different. My friend had become a Christian and I thought he was a bit daft, but I started going to Saturday night meetings with him and really enjoyed it. My faith in God grew gradually and life started getting better.

I trained as a sports instructor and was offered a job in Scotland. I was very nervous about going and prayed a lot about it, but just three hours after arriving in the hotel I met the only Christian working there out of 200 staff. He was called Mark and we became good friends. He had also dated the lady who was going to become my wife! I had seen Mary around, but it wasn't until we met in the post office, when I picked up money for her that she had dropped, that we got to know each other. We later found out the link with Mark. Mary became a Christian and we fell in love, married and had our first child, a son, in Scotland.

After five years I took a job in Wakefield as the manager of a hotel leisure club. We found a fantastic church almost by accident when I was walking through the town centre, but after two years, I took a promotion managing a sports centre back in Middlesbrough.

We started attending the Tees Valley Community Church and I met Gram again. I knew Gram from around town back in the 1980s, and had been told he had become homeless.

When I found out he'd become a Christian, I was intrigued.

Gram and I renewed our friendship, and before he started Sowing Seeds, he told me about the charity and asked me to pray for him.

I had left leisure management and started a business in recruitment consultancy. Gram asked me before Christmas in 2008 to become involved in Sowing Seeds, but I thought prison ministry would clash with my family life and business. However, the opportunity came up to be involved in helping to co-ordinate events and outreach activities, and by then the charity base was just five minutes away from my home. It was the right time to get involved.

Sometimes you don't always know why things happen the way they do. I couldn't have prevented my sister's death, but I can find some meaning to it. Strangely enough my dad died on 29 July 2007 – the morning of the anniversary of her death. Out of 365 days, it happened on exactly the same day. It nearly happened two weeks previously – in fact, the priest had given him the last rites and summoned my mum – but Dad held on. I believe it was God's confirmation to me that my sister and dad are both with Him.

But I also believe I'm still here for a reason, and if I'd have carried on with my life the way it was, I don't think I would be. At one time I was an angry and selfish person, and I believe you reap what you sow. My friend Jimmy, a Christian, told me that God had given him a vision of my gravestone, which would have become reality if I had continued in that way of life; we have seen that happen to so many people. But I was fortunate enough over many years to meet people who have helped me. Now I hope to help other people who need to find a hope and a better future. To live a life as a Christian is not an easy choice, but now, when I look back at my life over the past nineteen years, it has been fantastic. In the book of Isaiah chapter 43, verses 18–19 it says: 'Forget the former things; do not dwell on the past. See, I am doing a new thing! Now it springs up; do you not perceive it? I am making a way in the desert and streams in the wasteland.'

This scripture talks about the future and all that can be achieved if we trust God. Gram Seed is a great example, who is now doing great work and helping people to live with renewed hope.

TRUE FREEDOM

By Graham Bond (volunteer)

I have known Gram for about thirteen years, and soon realised his conversion was very real and truly miraculous. Despite many opportunities for pride and arrogance about what he has achieved, even to this day he remains humble and teachable, giving God all the glory for every good thing in his life.

It was mainly because of this that I was attracted to start working with him when he began his ministry to prisons. I lived quite close to Kirklevington Grange Prison and felt both my middle-class background and long-term Christian experience might work as an interesting contrast to Gram!

I have now been going into Kirklevington Grange once a week for the last nine years. I recall one period of about six months, when the only prisoners at the meetings were Muslims and we had some very interesting discussions regarding our faiths. From time to time we see men leave, having been dramatically saved. As I write this, it's been just a few weeks since a lifer in his forties, who had been in prison since he was a teenager, left to begin a new life as a completely changed man.

God has given me a real heart for prisoners and it has been a privilege to get alongside them and continue to help some of them once they have been freed. However, as we regularly remind them, true freedom is not about being out of jail; it's about living lives with Jesus at the centre.

CHAPTER NINE

REAPING THE REWARD

Stories of those supported by the team and transformed by the Lord.

NO GOING BACK

By Mark Owens

'No way, that's a load of rubbish,' I said, as I watched a 'Hell's Angel' evangelist praying for the crowd. I was fifteen years old and about to invite God into my life. But it didn't last long. It was going to take a long journey of pain, addiction, failed marriages, mental illness, suicide attempts and imprisonment before I would finally allow God back in again.

I'd been brought up in a Christian home and attended church, but I didn't believe any of it – until the night I met the American preacher. A former Hell's Angel, he was speaking at an event organised by the Billingham Pentecostal Church. My mum took me and I watched in disbelief as people started falling over when the preacher prayed for them.

'Why don't you go up and give your heart to Jesus,' my mum suggested.

I decided to give it a go and walked to the front. As soon as I was prayed for, I suddenly felt my legs start to go. I tried to stop it, but I ended up on the floor. I'll never forget that feeling – it was like a hosepipe had washed me out inside my body. It was amazing to feel so clean inside. I knew then that the Lord was real and I gave my heart to Him that day.

I started out well as a Christian and even went on a mission trip to Romania, smuggling Bibles and provisions into orphanages. But very soon I started distancing myself from God and living the kind of life that nearly destroyed me.

At seventeen I got married and joined the Parachute Regiment of the army. I left after three years and started kick boxing, gained my international title and spent six months fighting in Los Angeles. I was then scouted to become a professional boxer and for the next nine years I fought all over the country, alongside working the doors in Teesside. Throughout this time I still believed in God and often prayed, but I got heavily into drinking and womanising. I ended up wrecking two marriages – I had a breakdown after the first one and ended up at St Luke's Hospital, where Gram had been years before. In the end I had five children by four different women. By the time I was thirty I had started taking and selling drugs and neglecting my training – you have to be really dedicated as a professional and your manager brings you up a level each time, so you have a better chance of winning. But I was getting out of control and taking fights above my level. My last fight was way out of my league, and I ended up in hospital for six months in an induced coma with a blood clot on my brain. I was in a bad way and couldn't walk or talk. Some of the lads from the doors came and sat with me, including my friend Chris Crossan. He later became a Christian, but sometimes I would try and tell him about God and he would just smile at me.

It was a slow recovery and I had to learn to walk and talk again. But I could no longer get a licence to fight. I was gutted

– boxing had been my life and now I'd lost it. But instead of replacing the gap with God, I got worse. My drug taking increased, my personality changed dramatically to the point where one day I climbed up a lamppost wearing a notice that read 'public execution', and tried to hang myself. I had already phoned the police. I was taken to hospital and diagnosed as having psychotic episodes brought on by drink and drugs.

But worse than that, I started being violent towards my girlfriend, Jody. She was the love of my life and we had two children together. Even though she didn't share my beliefs, she kept asking me to take her to church, but I didn't want to. I'd fallen too far away from God.

Eventually social services got involved, wouldn't let me back to my house and took Jody and the children to a refuge. I ended up living in my friend's house and we got raided by police for dealing drugs. I was charged and while I was on bail I squatted in my old house. I totally hit rock bottom at that point; those were the worst days of my life. I was thirty-four and had lost everything: boxing, my home, my children and my girlfriend. I missed them so much and it broke my heart. I decided to hang myself again. My first attempt failed when a girl I knew suddenly decided to visit me. She found me hanging, pulled me down and called an ambulance. But I hadn't given up. As soon as I got out of hospital, I tried again. But this time the rafter in the loft snapped and I fell down, hit the banister and fractured my skull.

When Jody came out of the refuge, I followed her to Darlington and rented a flat. I started seeing her again, but we still argued and I hit another low point. I sat in my flat one night and injected heroin for the first time. I thought it would bring relief, but it was like a trip to hell. I felt so ill and saw horrific visions – I can't even begin to describe how bad it was. I haven't touched drugs since.

After six months I was back in court. It was my first offence, so I was only expecting a two-year suspended sentence, but the judge gave me four years. I nearly collapsed.

Arriving at Holme House I felt really down and missed everyone so much. Social services wouldn't let me see my children and told me that if I got back with Jody, the children would be taken away from us. But she had moved on by then and had started seeing someone else. That broke my heart even more, and I started getting murderous thoughts about her new boyfriend. Every night in my cell I went to sleep restless and disturbed, thinking about how to kill him.

I knew I had to come to a decision about my life. I could either go one way or the other, and I decided it was time to turn my life around. I cried out to God in despair, and that's when Gram came along. I first came across him when I was in St Luke's a few years previously. He had come to visit me, but I refused to see anyone and sent him away.

I knew this time I had to talk to him; I was so convinced I would commit murder as soon as I got out. But Gram listened to me and prayed for me. Those thoughts disappeared and I started sleeping properly for the first time since entering prison.

He gave me a copy of his book and I couldn't put it down – I think I read it in two days. It brought tears to my eyes at certain points because I was so happy for him and the way his life turned out. He had hit rock bottom, like me, and Jesus was still there for him and brought him back. I saw real hope in that book and it reminded me of the love Jesus has for us and the fact that He's there for us no matter how bad things get. As soon as I had finished the book, I got on my knees in my cell and cried out to God to be with me and walk with me. I felt His presence all the way through my sentence.

I decided to do everything I could to change my life. I

signed up for a twelve-month drug treatment programme, got clean, attended lots of courses to learn about relationships and anger management and studied counselling skills. Gram and Ian Williamson supported me all the way and the chaplains Sue, Graham and John were also brilliant.

I've also seen God change some of the hardest lads I've met in jail, and it's unbelievable. One of the lifers in another prison, Jay Richardson, writes to me every week and always puts a Bible verse on the envelope. His faith is amazing and he keeps reminding me that he's praying for me. It helps to give me more faith and strength.

After eighteen months I moved to Kirklevington Grange and finally got out of jail in summer 2009. I'm now working as general assistant for a chauffeur hire company, and I'm really grateful to Graham and Sonia (prison workers), who have made that possible. I'm also building up a fights promotion business with Chris Crossan – I can't be a boxer again, but I can be around the sport and help to put on shows. Social services have also written to me and told me I can see my children again.

I really wanted to find a girlfriend, but I knew it was over between me and Jody. I prayed about this and one day I saw a girl in a shop in town – at the time I was attending college from the open prison and was with one of the chaplains. The girl and I looked at each other, and I was just about to go and talk to her when Brian from Sowing Seeds walked past and offered us a lift. I still wanted to talk to the girl, but we needed to go back to prison, so I was really disappointed.

However, when we drove out of the car park, Brian's ticket wouldn't work in the exit barrier, so we had to go back to the ticket machine.

'Beauty, that!' I said to myself. I saw the girl again and she came running over and asked if she could have my number.

'No, but I'll have yours,' I told her. She's called Sinead and we've been together ever since!

My parents are really happy about the way my life is changing. They never stopped praying for me, but they were really ashamed when I went to prison and it was a big shock for them. I don't think they liked it when I'd got my first tattoo and then ended up covered in them! Then it was a baby here, another baby there, drink and drugs. They had to let me go and I made a right mess of it all. When you try to go your own way and get selfish, it all goes wrong. Gram's book shows that – when he was in control of his own life, he had nothing, but when God took control, it started to change and he's got a lovely life now.

I think it took a lot to admit what I was and what I'd become. I was a monster. It's a horrible thing to be violent in a relationship, and to face what I'd done was really hard. I've learned all the strategies now for avoiding those situations and I pray constantly, but I also had to learn to forgive myself and move on.

But thinking back to that night with the 'Hell's Angel', I know that what I felt was real and it's still here all those years later, despite what I've been through. Evil can get everywhere, but so can God. You can go into some of the worst places imaginable, but God will always be there for you. God's been with me all this time, even though I didn't realise it. I messed up, but I've put God in the driving seat now and I'm not the same person that went into prison. I know what God's done for me and I intend to stick with Him this time.

NEW BEGINNING

By Dan Hope

'If you have a boy, I'm leaving you,' my dad told my mum when she fell pregnant with me. He didn't like boys. As a young child he made sure I knew about it.

As soon as I was born, he started beating up my mum. My home became one of violence and fear. It upset me so much that I was often sent to stay with my grandma; my mum didn't want me to see what was happening.

My dad wasn't violent towards me, but he didn't seem to want much to do with me. The only thing he ever bought me was a pair of trainers. He made promises to me and never kept them. I didn't trust him. The only person I trusted was my grandma.

My sister was born when I was four and seemed to get much more from my dad, being a girl. He had left my mum by this time.

Grandma went to church regularly and took me with her, but I didn't really believe in God. Then, when I was six, my mum started taking me to church. She met someone there who seemed to me to be a bit of a nutcase; it was his first time in church, and when the music came on he started dancing at the back. He soon became Mum's new boyfriend.

He helped to look after me, but for years I didn't like him, especially when he started disciplining me. The first time was when I pushed my sister off her bike – he hit me round the back of the head. I wasn't used to that authority – I'd been the man of the house up until then. I wanted to be the boss and have my own way, like I'd had with my grandma.

Mum married her boyfriend when I was eight and asked if I wanted to have his surname and call him Dad. I said yes, even though I was still wary of him. He was in the Royal Marines and had a lifestyle of fighting and drinking. Eventually I grew to like him and tried to impress him by fighting, because that was what I'd seen him do. He wasn't impressed, but he told me he didn't mind the police coming to the house because I'd been fighting, but he did mind if it was for something else. I grew up thinking it was OK to fight. There were times, though, when I was simply getting back at someone who had hurt me; once at secondary school a lad threw me across a table and injured my back. The bottom of my spine had already been damaged when I had fallen on a toy tractor as a child, and this made it worse. I hated the lad for months, but didn't dare do anything. One day, he made a passing comment and I flipped and whacked him. He didn't return to school the following term.

We moved house and I started at a new school, but it didn't stop me fighting – in fact, I had a fight on my first day at school. When I left I decided to join the Royal Marines, but turned down my place in the end because my girlfriend asked me not to go. We split up a few weeks later. Instead of the Marines, I did a construction apprenticeship in groundwork and was offered a job in my friend's construction company.

But the one thing I had a real yearning for was getting my driving licence and a car; I thought it would somehow solve all my problems. I also remembered the thrill of going to my grandma and granddad's caravan as a child – my uncle used to sit me on his knee and drive around the site. I loved it. By the time I was fourteen, I decided to try it for myself. My grandma was working as a cook at the local church and one day when she wasn't looking, I took the car keys out of her bag and sneaked into her car. I tried to put it in reverse, but only managed to get it into first gear and it shot into a ditch. She wasn't happy, to say the least!

She paid for my driving lessons when I was seventeen, and as soon as I got my first car, I felt like the bee's knees. I drove everywhere with my mates and often took off somewhere quiet on my own if I felt stressed. It was even better when I was nineteen and got my new MG. It was the best thing that had ever happened to me.

I could afford it, even though I was blowing a lot of money on fruit machines. I had three jobs by then: the building work, my mum's off licence and working on the doors. Being a bouncer also gave me licence to fight and a bit of power; in fact, my boss would praise me every time I had a fight.

But then my world started to fall apart; my grandma was diagnosed with ovarian cancer. She managed to fight it at first, but it soon came back and I was told there wasn't much hope for her. She was everything to me and I had no idea how I would manage without her. She went into a hospice and I visited her every day. I didn't quite understand the implications though; I thought it was just a normal hospital.

The pain of all this was too great, and I suddenly became a lunatic driver. Speed and danger became an addiction and I got a buzz from racing other cars, shooting through red lights and driving on the wrong side of the road. In the end, other cars wouldn't race me because I was so crazy; those who would gave up after a while. Even police were targets. I'd spot a police car, flick a few finger gestures and fly off, hoping that they would chase me. Nine times out of ten they did.

But when grandma finally died it was game over for me. Everything had gone and nothing mattered any more. But the strange thing was that on the day she died, something triggered in my mind and I began driving sensibly. But it didn't stop the tragedy that was about to happen.

Two weeks after my grandma's death, I took a couple of friends to see a car one of them was going to buy, and on the way back we drove on a two-lane road that merged into a single lane. There was an old lady driving in the outside lane, trying to get into the inside lane before it merged and a young lad driving in front wouldn't let her in. I felt so angry at him and decided to show him who was boss.

I overtook him and then he did the same to me. This carried on for a while until he got fed up and drove off. Suddenly, the traffic lights in front of me changed to red. I couldn't stop in time and shot straight through. At that point, a man ran across the road and I swerved to avoid him. But it was too late. I hit him and he smashed through the windscreen, snapping his spine. His blood was all over us and shards of glass were everywhere. My mates were crying and in shock. At that point I panicked and drove off. I dropped off my friends at the side of the road so that they wouldn't get into trouble – it was my fault after all – and parked the car. I pulled my socks over my tracksuit bottoms, put on a hat from my car and started running as if I was out jogging. A police officer drove past, turned round at the roundabout and put his lights on. I thought he'd spotted me, so I started running through gardens and jumping over fences to escape. Eventually I ran into a pub and phoned my mum.

'Mum, I've done something really bad. I need to leave the country,' I told her.

'I'll come and get you,' she said. As soon as she arrived I told her I needed to go to the police station; it must have been the sense of guilt. I also called my friends and told them to do the same and to tell the truth.

When I handed myself in, I found out that the man I'd hit had died. I broke down in tears. He was fifty-one, but for some reason I had thought he was a young lad because of the way he ran across the road. I was at the police station for twenty hours altogether, being interviewed by the murder squad and traffic police. When I was released on bail, I met my friends in the pub and told them what had happened. But as I talked about it, all the pain and shock came back and the drink wasn't enough to get rid of it. My mate suggested taking some cocaine. It was my first time, but it worked and I took it every day after that. The flat I'd moved into above my parents' off licence became like a drug den. My drinking also increased and I went from drinking two litres of cider a day to about nine litres.

I was so full of remorse that when I met my barrister, I asked him if there was any way I could show the family how sorry I was for what had happened. He said there was nothing I could do.

'What if I ask to go to prison now?' I said.

'But you won't get sentenced for another year,' he told me.

'It's what I want.' He asked the judge if it could be arranged, and I became the first man in the country to ask to go to prison.

The day arrived and I stood there in the dock, blanking everyone out. I fixed my eyes on the judge; if I'd looked at my friends and family, it would have upset me and I couldn't bear to look at the family of the man I'd killed.

I was sentenced to five years and taken to YOI Castington. I was just nineteen years old. The night before the court appearance, I'd taken so many different drugs and drunk so much that for the first two days in prison, I was still high and drunk.

My mate, for some reason, dared me to not cut my hair or shave until I got out. I went along with it and remained in that state for months, until Gram came to see me. I thought he was so nice and really wanted him to come and see me again. But it had another effect; after I met him I went back to the wing and had a haircut and a shave. I suddenly wanted to be smart on the outside as well as happy on the inside.

I decided to make the best of life inside and got a job in the kitchens. I didn't fight or do anything wrong, and because of that, I ended up working in the staff mess; I was the first prisoner ever to do so.

I was still troubled by what I'd done, but I was serving out my punishment, so it made it easier to cope. I knew the story had been in the local papers, and once I saw myself on the news. Apparently I was the ninth person in the country to knock someone over that year. I turned the TV off straight away.

Gram visited me several times and I always knew there was something different about him. I didn't understand how someone could change so much, but I didn't think it was anything to do with God.

The governor asked me which prison I wanted to go to, and I asked to go to Kirklevington Grange, which was an open prison, meaning I could be let out during the day. However, before I left Castington I got really fed up and was missing my family, so I kicked off and started swearing at the kitchen staff. I was sacked and thought I'd blown everything. I was allowed to go, but on the way, there was a phone call to say my place had been taken by someone else. I was so disappointed. I was taken to Holme House, but they couldn't accept me because I was assigned to a different prison.

Once that was resolved, I was allowed into Holme House. But it was a man's jail and I was terrified.

'Don't worry,' said my mum. 'Gram goes in there, you'll be all right.' It wasn't as bad as I'd expected and was actually better than Castington. By the time I managed to get to Kirklevington, I was allowed to attend college, where I trained as a hairdresser.

I served two and a half years altogether, but when I got

out, the guilt and shame of what I had done came flooding back. Three days after release I started on cocaine again. I had met someone at work and we moved in together and had a baby, but not even becoming a dad stopped me going off the rails. I got sacked from my hairdressing job for becoming lazy, and three months before my second child was born, I was spending up to £300 a night on drugs.

I knew I needed to stop – something in my head was telling me to. Around that time I attended a meeting about the halfway house that Sowing Seeds had set up. There were a lot of complaints about it in the area, and I had been working for some time in a nearby barber's shop. I wanted to get the point across that everyone had treated me as normal, even though I was a criminal – why couldn't they do the same for the lads in the house?

After that meeting, I approached Gram and asked if I could talk to him. We had a coffee together and talked about my addiction. He said that behind every addiction there's always a problem. I told him I thought losing my grandma was still affecting me. He understood; he'd gone through the same thing.

I spent more time with him and he invited me to join him on various trips. But I was still taking drugs and seemed to be getting worse. One day he started talking about Jesus. I had stopped going to church when I was a teenager – I wanted to drink, smoke and hang about with my friends instead. But I still remembered something my granddad had told me when I was a child: 'People don't believe in God because you can't see Him, but you can't see the wind, yet you believe it's there and you feel it.'

I wanted to be like Gram. I knew he had something different. His friends were nice and mine just wanted me to fight and take drugs.

He invited me to go with him to a Welsh church, where he was giving a talk. I didn't take anything or drink for a few days beforehand and didn't suffer any withdrawal symptoms. I wanted to be nice and fresh for going away. But it was more than that – I didn't actually want to. I felt happy.

As I listened to Gram speaking at the church about Jesus, I really believed what he was saying. The church was packed with drug addicts and alcoholics. I looked around at them.

'They really need help,' I said to myself. Then it struck me; so did I.

The next day in the Sunday service, Gram asked anyone who wanted to receive Jesus to put their hands out. I decided at that point that I was sick of my old life and it wasn't going to hurt me to try something different. I put my hands out and suddenly felt weird, like my body was tingling. Gram asked me if I'd ever asked Jesus into my heart and I said I hadn't, but that I wanted to. As I did, I felt warm and fresh and all the pain in my heart just disappeared. I knew I was different.

I helped Gram to pray for others, which was something new. I'd only ever prayed for myself before, usually asking God to get me out of bad situations or to give me something I wanted.

But back at home I fell at the first hurdle – I got stoned with my brother. However, it wasn't the same and I didn't enjoy it. I started feeling really paranoid at every sound – creaking doors, the sound of the wind, barking dogs. Afterwards, I read the Ten Commandments in the Bible and thought that if I believed in Jesus, I had to do what He told me to. But it wasn't that easy. I hadn't touched cocaine since becoming a Christian, but I think my brother hadn't accepted my beliefs and assumed we'd carry on doing what we'd always done. It became a vicious cycle. I'd smoke skunk, pray for forgiveness in the morning and then do it again the next night. The devil wanted to keep hold of me and I didn't know how to get out of it.

One morning, I woke up and there was something in my head saying, 'You need to stop this, son. It's no good for you.' I believe it was Jesus speaking to me.

But life is so much better than it was. I spend time with Gram most days. My passion is football and I'm going to take coaching badges to work with local kids. I'm also playing for a church team. I'm getting married soon and my fiancée comes to church with me. I still miss my grandma, but now I know she's in heaven and one day I'll see her again. All the guilt and pain has been taken away by Jesus.

REDEMPTION

By Chris Crossan (Bram)

If it wasn't for Gram's book I think I'd be doing a long stretch in prison by now. I had my heart set on revenge – and I didn't care if I got caught.

I'd always been a fighter and I had gained a reputation for being one of the hard men in Teesside. I ran wild for a long time and injured a lot of people, but underneath it all I was really just a frightened little kid trying to make sure no one would ever hurt me again.

Life was tough right from the beginning. My mum had an affair and became pregnant with me. Although her husband stayed with her, he treated me really badly as a young boy and was violent towards both my mum and me. My mum and her husband split up and Mum fell apart. She tried to commit suicide and I found her after she'd slit her wrists. I was about three at the time.

Eventually she remarried and had two more children. At

first everything was fine, but soon my stepdad also became violent towards me – he would pin me down and order the other kids to hit me. I became so angry and determined that no one else would ever do that to me again. I had to learn to look after myself.

I became a violent teenager and started hanging around with people who took drugs, and took them myself – ecstasy, amphetamines, cocaine, crack. I also took up boxing and karate, which kept me out of trouble for a while, but also made me better at street fighting.

There were a lot of people on the scene that I looked up to. They had money, nice cars, a powerful reputation and I had nothing – I had to go boxing in a pair of jeans because they were the only trousers I owned. I wanted to be like them, even though some are now doing life sentences. They may have been bad, but they were also like a family. Being part of that firm I felt like I belonged and I was protected. But I still felt under threat – sometimes I'd sleep with a gun under my bed.

Two major incidents really affected me. When I was seventeen, a man ran me over and hit me with an axe. I turned really wild after that and went back to fight the man a couple of weeks later. Then, when I was twenty-one, I was seriously injured again in a street fight. I was hit with bats and ended up with a bleed in my brain the size of a tennis ball. I nearly died, and while I was unconscious, I saw a vision of my granddad and a lad I knew from school who had died. It was white and peaceful and I wanted to be with them. Somehow I managed to come out of it and they brought me round.

But near death didn't make any difference to my behaviour. My mum was hoping it would.

'Surely you are going to change now after this?' she pleaded.

'No, I'm not!' I shouted at her. I expected that I would end up getting killed – I think I wanted to, if I'm honest. I wasn't happy with my life. I just wanted to be put out of my misery.

But something happened that made me want to sort myself out: I became a dad for the second time. I'd already had a child a few years previously, but I ruined the relationship. This time I really wanted to sort myself out. I stopped taking drugs, which was really hard. But my efforts didn't last long. One evening I had an argument with someone over money. We were in a moving car at the time and I got so angry that I threw the man out. I had no idea whether he was alive or dead.

I had to escape, so I went on the run to Tenerife. While waiting at the airport, I met Dan Hope's dad, Eddie May, who is a Christian. He talked to me about his faith. We met up in Tenerife and continued talking. While we were walking around a local market, I saw a picture of Jesus on sale on one of the stalls. I felt compelled to buy it; it seemed to represent my desperation to change and find hope and faith. As I spent time with Eddie, we talked a lot about Jesus. I did have a belief of sorts; in fact I used to read the Bible as a child. What Eddie said really touched me and I decided to return to England and sort myself out.

The first time I realised something had changed was when I was having a meal in a restaurant one night and someone was staring at me with a strange look on his face. I was angry; I had my knife ready.

'If he looks at me like that again, I'm going to stab him.' I suddenly realised I had said it out loud and he came over. I don't know why but I suddenly threw the knife away, ran outside and burst into tears. I cried for what felt like hours. But something was different in me after this and I stopped taking drugs, started training properly, got a job on the doors and stopped all criminal activity. Life continued to improve, and a couple of years later I was competing in jujitsu competitions in Brazil and won a couple of European titles. But once again, my life started to fall apart. I found out my girlfriend had been unfaithful to me when I was in Brazil and it really cracked me up. I started running wild again, but this time it was worse. I had new fighting skills and I was dangerous. I patched things up with my girlfriend and we had another baby. I tried to sort myself out yet again and opened a gym. I let a lot of the young lads train for free – they reminded me of myself when I was young. Now some of them are making a real success of their lives so I finally felt like I'd done something good.

For a couple of years, I ran gyms in different places and also promoted mixed match shows, shows which include different types of fighting. But by this time I really hated drug dealers with a passion and started to rob and scam them. I also got another girl pregnant – someone who trained in my gym. Even though she was the mother of my child, the relationship didn't work out. But then my lowest point came. Somebody committed a crime so sick and low that I became determined to seek revenge the only way I knew how. I had never felt this bad before, but this time no one was going to stop me.

It was at this point that my friend Mark Owens gave me a copy of *One Step Beyond* after he'd read it in prison. As soon as I started reading it, I broke down in tears. A voice inside me seemed to be saying, 'Phone Gram.'

'I can't do that,' I said to myself. 'He will think I'm a maniac if I tell him I'm hearing voices.' But in the end, I decided to call him – his number was in the book. There was no answer, so I sent him a text, telling him what had happened.

He asked me to meet him and I told him what I was planning to do.

'If I don't do this I will feel like I'm a coward,' I told him.

'But it's the devil who wants you to do this,' he said. I knew he was right.

He invited me to church where I gave my life to Jesus, was baptised in the Holy Spirit and started speaking in tongues straight away. I was on such a high that I didn't want to leave the place and I could hardly eat because I felt so full – it was indescribable. At that point, it was hard to believe what I was planning to do a couple of days previously.

Since then there have been a lot of trials and temptations, and if it wasn't for Gram's support, I would have really struggled. But I've managed to keep following God. I don't want to be the person I was any more; I want to do good and not bad and I don't want to let Gram down either. It's been life changing; I've met so many nice people in the Christian community, and people like me don't really know that they exist.

I still run a security business and I'm involved in cage fighting, which is a mixture of different types of fighting. I'm really excited about that. I've also just opened a new gym to allow kids like I used to be, without hope and without money, to train for free again. I had to commit crime to get money for things I wanted and I don't want others to feel that they have to do the same. I also want to provide something that kids can put their aggression into, such as sport. The gym is called Redemption, which speaks for itself really. I want local kids to recognise that bad really is bad and being good is so much better and gives them a more successful life.

However, I felt very unworthy as a new Christian because of all the bad things I'd done. I was planning to get baptised in the River Swale, Richmond, but I felt so nervous and unsure because of my past. While I was agonising over this, I looked on the Facebook website and saw something written by a world-class fighter, Jorge Rivera, who's a Christian; he was talking about a river full of saved souls. It really spoke to me and I went ahead with the baptism, which was fantastic.

But I would like to be strong, be surrounded by angels and not have to street fight any more. I just wanted to stop people hurting me in the beginning, but I feel sick when I think of some of the things I've done. I also want to be a good role model to my children, like Gram's been a good role model to me. I don't want them to have the life that I had. I have now put my past behind me and thanks to Jesus I can look forward. I've also met a wonderful Christian girl called Heidi and now I can enjoy my new life and I'm really happy. We're getting married on 10 October 2009 at All Saints Church, Eaglescliffe.

So many people have read Gram's book and it's had a massive impact. My friend is a traveller, who struggles with reading and had never read a book in his life. He read Gram's book in two days! It's really anointed. It saved my life.

> *'Remember not the sins of my youth and my rebellious ways; according to your love remember me, for you are good, O LORD.'*
>
> Psalm 25, verse 7

BORN AGAIN BEN

By Ben Falaja (boxer sponsored by Sowing Seeds Ministries)

The day I experienced the powerful presence of God for the first time, I was accused of being on drugs! I'd never had the courage to go into a place like that before. I had wanted to in the past, but was scared of rejection – something I'd faced for most of my life.

140

I'd been invited to church, along with a couple of other lads, and it hit me as soon as I walked in the door. It was overwhelming.

'Wow! Can you feel that?' I said to the lads.

'What on earth have you been taking?' they responded, looking at me suspiciously. For once it wasn't the drugs.

I didn't know much about Christianity up until then. The only time I had been told anything was when a local preacher came into our primary school and talked about Jesus. I remember having an overwhelming feeling in my heart that He was real. I didn't have any idols growing up, but I thought it would be amazing to be like Jesus.

Growing up in a rough area of Middlesbrough, my only role models were the drug dealers and fighters I hung around with as a young teenager. They were respected and accepted, something I craved. I thought I needed to be like them in order to gain acceptance.

Those feelings of rejection had been in me for a long time. My dad lived in London and never came to see me or my sister. Not having a father figure was really hard on me, especially at events like football matches when he wasn't there to watch me play. It seemed like all the other dads were there, apart from mine. Many times I used to sit in my bedroom in tears, crying out, 'Dad, why aren't you here for me?' I think without realising it I was crying out to another Father – one that I now know.

There were a lot of rough families and crime in the area, and being a young, dark-skinned lad, especially without a dad around, they found me an easy target. Sometimes kids wouldn't let me play football with them because of the colour of my skin. When I told my mum she would say, 'Get back out there – it's a free country!' It gave me a strong spirit and kept me going, especially when it got tough. However, I grew up carrying a lot of anger and hatred, fighting and lashing out all the time. By the time I was thirteen I started to take and sell drugs, go to raves and hang around the streets drinking. I was disruptive in lessons and used to smoke weed before going into school. I wasn't happy. I felt trapped, desperate and couldn't see a way out.

I left school without qualifications, but trained as a plumber. Around this time I started thinking about life and death and whether God was real or not. I had decided as a child that He existed, after praying and seeing things happen. The first time was when I had got dirty after playing out and asked my mum if I could have a bath. She said no.

'God, I pray that next time I ask, she will say yes.' I asked again and she let me have a bath. I believed He was real then. Mind you, I also used to pray for a motorbike, but I didn't get one, which was probably for my own good!

Desperate for answers, sometimes I would stop outside churches when I'd been smoking weed and drinking. For a moment I would sober up and sense someone or something telling me to go in. I never did. I thought everyone would look at me and think I was up to no good, because of the colour of my skin. I didn't want to risk any more rejection.

In the end I cried out to God, saying, 'If you are there, God, will You do something significant that I can't ignore to bring me back to reality?'

Something big did happen, something that I won't forget until the day I die. My nana went into hospital for three days with a bowel problem. I was getting ready to visit her and as soon as I set foot in the house I had an overwhelming feeling of what I now believe was the Holy Spirit, telling me my prayers had been answered. I knew something was very wrong and my cousin arrived, saying my nana was on a life support machine and not expected to live. I rushed to the hospital to be with her and she was there, attached to wires and drips, looking at me. I told her I loved her, and then they turned the machine off. She was only sixty-five. I looked at her lying there and she seemed so peaceful. It hit me hard. I thought there had to be more to life than just death.

After Nana died, I joined a local boxing gym and met a man there called Tony Grange. Unknown to me at the time, Tony was a Christian and had been praying about whether he should give up boxing. God gave him a vision in which he was singing a hymn and there was a line of people in front of him. Suddenly, a dark lad with a big smile stepped out of the line and started singing the hymn with him. He believed that God was saying he was going to bring people in, but there were no black lads in the gym at that time – until I joined.

We went for a meal and he told me about his faith. I talked about what I had been going through and he invited me and a couple of other lads to his church. God's presence was so amazing that night that I knew without a doubt that He was real. I publicly gave my life to God right then, at the age of eighteen.

I was very much involved in boxing by then, but was losing a lot of fights. I prayed about it and God said, 'The more you give up to Me, the more I will bless you in this sport.' I stopped taking drugs, drinking, going out, spending time with women, and soon I was winning titles and represented my country. God really started to bless me, and I've achieved so much because of it. I progressed from novice to intermediate to open class in four years. In boxing that's unheard of. I box for England now.

Sowing Seeds Ministries have sponsored my boxing, and I've got their logo on my shorts – in fact, some people call me Born Again Ben, so I'm having that sewn into my shorts as well!

Gram invited me to share my testimony in Hassockfield and Castington YOI. I go in regularly and tell the youngsters how God's changed my life. I've met a lot of people I know in prison. They can't believe I'm there because I am a Christian, rather than because I've been caught!

In the end I'm just a pawn, and willing to be moved where God wants me. But I still find it amazing when I think about where I was and how God has carried me through and changed my life.

CHAPTER TEN

COMMUNITY SPIRIT

Supporters of Sowing Seeds Ministries:

POLICE SERGEANT BRIAN MCCARTHY
Cleveland Police

> ... *there's something very powerful about an ex-con baptising a policeman. It's really spoken to the lads in the prison ...*
>
> Gram Seed, *One Step Beyond*

The first time I met Gram, what I saw was a happy but harmless drunk lingering in a fish and chip shop. I had received a call on my radio one evening that a 6ft 5 bloke had been causing havoc, and suddenly I spotted him a few feet away, walking across a nearby roundabout. I had to go and deal with him.

'How do you use this thing then?' he slurred, taking my baton out of its holder.

'Gimme it back and I'll show you,' I told him. He did and I put it away. 'You won't be seeing that again!'

I sent him on his way, but when I eventually read about his violence in *One Step Beyond*, I turned cold. I was glad I had handled him in the way I had. A while later I had to send him to prison for shoplifting.

When I met Gram again a few years later, he looked emaciated and skeletal because he'd been ill and in a coma, but there was a real glow about him. Then he started telling me about Jesus.

'Flipping heck, mate. You've been brainwashed,' I said to myself. I asked Gram, 'What have these people been saying to you?' I didn't see him again for another ten years.

Around the time Gram became a Christian, I visited my friend Keith Howard, who had also just become a Christian, and he told me about his faith. It was ten years before I gave my life to the Lord and when I attended the church that Keith went to, I immediately saw Gram with his family! I couldn't believe it; of all the churches I chose to go to, he was there. Gram was baptising new Christians that weekend and I asked if he would baptise me too. I thought it would be a nice way to seal the fact that he's on this new journey and I was starting on mine.

Gram's testimony is just amazing, and reading his book coloured in the whole picture for me, because like a lot of people I wasn't fully aware of everything that he'd been through. A number of police have read the book and they are amazed by the story too.

I'm now the branch leader for the Christian Police Association for Cleveland Police – an organisation that started 125 years ago, caring for overworked officers and their families, which aims to bring the love of God to the police force. I facilitate community action between the churches and the police, but I'm also there for my colleagues when they need help. I've obtained a lot of New Testaments and Psalms for police officers, and Gram has provided me with large-print Bibles which are now in the custody offices, for those that are locked up after arrest but might not have their glasses with them. I now have permission from the Chief Constable to place copies of *One Step Beyond* in custody offices in Cleveland, which includes Middlesbrough, Stockton, Langbaurgh district and Hartlepool.

I feel for a lot of the people I deal with. I grew up in Glasgow on the biggest council estate in Europe, and I know a good few kids with good hearts that have turned to drugs and crime. Tragically, some of them died. We all have a choice and some go down the wrong path and never come off it. I want to see these people have hope that there is a better way.

But one thing that has struck me about the response to Gram's book is the realisation of who is actually on trial. In the Bible when Pontius Pilate was questioning Jesus, it wasn't really Jesus who was on trial, it was Pontius Pilate. That's the funny thing about the book; it's not Gram who's on trial, it's the person reading the book. Gram doesn't have to prove himself – the truth is evident about his life – but it's the impact it has on those reading the book. They then have a choice; they can either accept that truth or reject it.

DAN HOWARD

Manager of Powerleague Stockton

I've known Gram for some time now coming down here with his sons and having meetings with other Christians. The dramatic transformation in him is amazing. I read his book and absolutely loved it. It would be easy to think it's all a little far fetched, but since I've got to know him, I know that it's the complete truth. A lot of our customers knew Gram years ago and they won't accept it – they believe a guy like that can't change so much. One customer used to

IT MUST BE LOVE

be a security officer in one of the Middlesbrough shops and had a couple of run-ins with Gram. She didn't believe any of it until she met him. Now she says that it is true and it's unbelievable. A lot of the other parents were unsure at first, but now the crowds around him on a Saturday morning are getting bigger all the time.

For me personally, I'm asking Gram more questions about his beliefs and I go to church and listen more carefully to what's being said. His story has changed people.

PHIL LONGHURST

**Free Church Chaplain (Assemblies of God),
HMYOI Castington**

When *One Step Beyond* came out, we had a queue of young people wanting the book. They all loved it. Even those who can't read very well have been really gripped by it; it's amazing to think that someone who can hardly read can pick up this book and enjoy it. Some of the teachers in the prison have also used it in lessons to encourage the young people to read. We use the *One Step Beyond* DVD with our induction groups; the story brings a reality for them that God can help them within their similar 'hopeless' situations.

Sowing Seeds Ministries has such an important role in linking lads in here to the outside world. We get a lot of young people here from Hassockfield Secure Unit, and it means there's a link that carries on once they leave prison – the time when they can easily go astray. It's one thing having the theory of what we believe, but Sowing Seeds is the practice, and we really value their input here.

CHAPTER ELEVEN

WE ARE FAMILY

LIFE WITH GRAM

By Natasha Seed

'I thought you were dead!' the stranger said to my husband, looking completely stunned. I was rather stunned too – we were just shopping for a bed!

But shopping expeditions were never straightforward with Gram. When I first moved up to Middlesbrough as a young wife, Gram and I couldn't walk through the town for ten minutes without being spotted and stopped by someone who knew him. It's not much different nowadays, especially since *One Step Beyond* came out – because of this, I've even been recognised when I've been on my own. I don't really like being in the spotlight, however – I'd rather be in the background.

But despite all the challenges we've had, life with Gram is all I've ever wanted and I love what I have now.

When I met Gram in 1998, I had only been a Christian for nine months. My sister-in-law had become a Christian, but up until then I was focused on the London life – drinking, smoking and taking speed. I didn't want to give up my lifestyle and I thought becoming a Christian was quite a boring thing to do. But my sister-in-law's change was affecting my family – my brother, who was a bit of an atheist up until then, got saved and I saw the change in him. Next it happened to my sister. But it took another three years for me to become interested. At the time I still thought I was enjoying myself – I had my own flat and two jobs – but everything started to seem pointless. I didn't want to give up my lifestyle, but it began to feel really mundane – same old, same old. I also really wanted to get married and have children, but I wasn't going to meet anybody in the places I was going to. Life was going steadily downhill.

When I met up with my sister and sister-in-law and they told me about Jesus, I used to think that they were bonkers! They seemed really happy, but I thought they were making it up and pretending to be happy. The truth was that it was me who was pretending to be happy. I wanted what they had, and eventually gave my life to the Lord and gave up everything I knew that was wrong.

I ran a café with my mum for about two years until she had an asthma attack, went into a coma and was put on life support. Often, I would go to the hospital and find my brother and sister there praying for her. Even though I wasn't saved at that point, it gave me strength to think that God could be there for my mum in this time of need. She pulled through and we sold the café a week before I met Gram. He was visiting the church I was going to while he attended evangelism school.

The moment I saw him, the Lord spoke to me and said, 'That's your husband.' I didn't question it, but I didn't make any effort to talk to him or flirt with him either. I said to

God, 'If this is really from you, then let him give me his phone number.' He did, but he didn't really know why he was doing it!

We dated for just two months before he proposed, on my birthday. It was a bit of a whirlwind – I was both scared and excited. I lived in Essex, and Middlesbrough seemed like the other end of the world! I knew it was right to move up to his area, which was where God had called him to work.

It was tough at first, being in such a different culture. I missed my family and friends, and Gram and I were still getting to know each other. There was also the problem of his past. I had never known him as the old Gram, only the person he had become. We used to be followed around town and often we'd hear on security guards' radios: 'Gram Seed's in the shop!' Sometimes they even thought we were shoplifting and putting things in Caleb's pram. Once we were in a store and someone ran in, grabbed a load of stuff and ran off. Gram said we needed to stay where we were in case the police thought we were involved. I'd never lived that kind of life before.

We didn't have two pennies to rub together; I had about £100 in my pocket and a Ford Fiesta and Gram had nothing but his pushbike. We had to borrow a cot when we had Caleb. But I knew that was the way it was meant to be and it was where the Lord wanted us. We've been so blessed since then and Gram's ministry has gone from strength to strength. I love the work he does and I love the fact that he loves what he does.

Being involved in the ministry has not always been easy, though. Often we used to arrange to meet people every Sunday and most Sundays they wouldn't turn up.

'Gram, why do we have to keep doing this?' I kept saying to him.

'One day they will turn up,' was his response.

I see my role as being there for our boys, but also to offer hospitality. You have to be ready to have your house and your life invaded, but I don't mind. I love to see the changes in people's lives and I'm really happy to open up our home.

Living by faith has been tough, not always knowing where the money is going to come from, but Gram has taken the lead with that and has a very strong faith. The Lord has always given me peace about this and I've never really worried about it.

And now I don't feel so much of an outsider where we live. Middlesbrough is home, and although I'm not from here, I'm settled and happy. I know this is how it was meant to be. It would be nice to have a bit more support, but considering what we've gone through, it's not a violin story. We've muddled through. I love my life and being with the boys, and I wouldn't swap it for anything. Patrick Hinton used to tell us that the Lord put us together and the Lord doesn't make mistakes.

CHAPTER TWELVE

FREEDOM BEHIND BARS

The following extracts are from letters and emails received by Sowing Seeds Ministries and CWR from prisoners who have read *One Step Beyond*. No full names have been used so as to protect identities.

Dear Sir/Madam,
I am a fifteen-year-old boy who has met Gram and read his book, *One Step Beyond*. I was very touched by it and it has helped me turn my life around. I am trying to help others turn their lives around. I am going to church every Sunday. I may have done wrong, but now I am doing things right. I am a kid in care, so I can help people more and understand them. It would mean a lot if you wrote back.
J, West Yorkshire

Dear Gram,

Hi there, brother! I hope you don't mind me getting in touch with you. I've just finished reading your book and felt the urge to write to you straight away. Your story has really touched my heart. Sometimes when I read a book it can take me two to three days to finish it, depending on how I feel, but for some reason, I couldn't put yours down until I'd read it from page to page. I tried to put it down as I wanted to watch a film on TV, but it was impossible for me to do this. I was truly captivated! We have both led similar lives and I was with you nearly 100 per cent of the way and I truly mean this. To me, if I was lying, it wouldn't be worth saying that last sentence.

I have been in and out of prison since 1996. By the time I'm released from this sentence, I'll have spent around nine years inside Her Majesty's establishments, something that I'm not proud of talking about. I've let so many people down over the years, including myself, my family and not forgetting God and Jesus. I had to be kicked into touch. Like you, I should've been dead long ago. But I now realise God has other plans for my life. He hasn't finished with me yet and never would be. I also know that I wouldn't have got this far in life without him; for this I am more than grateful.

A, Leicestershire

Dear Gram,

Hi there and God bless you. I had to write to you after reading your book, *One Step Beyond*. It's amazing seeing and reading how God changed your life. I have read many books about people being saved by Jesus, which is marvellous. Yours well and truly touched me in mind, body and soul.

I was a man in so deep with alcohol myself. It was killing

me slowly and I lost everything and every person around me. A few years ago, I asked Jesus into my life and, wow, what an experience! I always thought Jesus was for nutters and crackpots, never for me.

I read your book in a couple of days and, man, I never cry. But through your book I cried and cried and prayed for you. Thank you for keeping it real.

With God's love

J. Norfolk

Book Review

After reading Gram Seed's book a couple of us girls got together and discussed it. We think that it really encourages people who have offended to see a better picture for their future and believe in themselves.

We think Gram is a really good role model to children in the prison and after we all read the book it proved to us that although we have nothing and no qualifications we can all do something with ourselves and when we all get out we all said that we want to prove not only to our families, but to everyone, that we can change just the way Gram proved it.

When we got together one of the girls said that she wanted to live her life in and out of prisons because that's all she'd ever done, but when she read the book she also said it make her think twice about it and she's now got plans to have a fresh start and start college.

Gram's book is very detailed and it goes deep into Gram's life and we all think that he has had a shocking life and everyone who has read the book in the prison were pleased to read the end of the book where he changed his life around.

Girls' prison group, County Durham

Dear Gram

I hope you remember me. Well, what made me want to write was that I completed reading your book last night and I just wanted to say it really made me think about becoming a Christian. Jesus really gave you the strength to become a better person. I would love to have him in my life to help me change. I am going to the chapel this Sunday. I am really looking forward to it! I prayed last night on my own for the first time and it really made me feel a lot better. Today has been a very good day after I prayed. Since I met you, you have inspired me. Thank you for everything you have done.

J, Northumberland

Hello Gram,

I read your book and was moved to hear your story. I was moved in my spirit to write to you and say I was inspired and touched. I also like what you're doing with your charity. I know leaving prison is not a nice experience and recognise that others as well as myself are short on direction.

One day I would hope to be able to be in a position to offer a helping hand to prisoners on release, Christ willing. Thanks for your inspiration (in the Lord, of course).

C, Birmingham

Dear Gram,

I'm writing because I want to congratulate you on your hard work and determination to see good in others, and of course giving me the opportunity to read your story.

I have read many books during my sentence but none as thought provoking as yours. I grew up in Middlesbrough and could relate to many of the places, including the bench.

Reading your story has made me cry, laugh and most importantly stopped me being a victim and have faith in myself and others.

I'm going to the chapel for the first time on Sunday after using many excuses not to go over a lot of months and I hope to listen, learn, understand and hopefully have a bond with God similar to yours one day.

Many thanks

S, Morpeth

Dear Gram,

Hi there Gram, I just thought I would drop you a letter to say that I have read your book and I think it was an excellent book to read. Thanks for the book and it's the best one I have read for a long time. I am thinking of all the bad things that happened to you and every time I go to church I always say a prayer for you.

Yours sincerely

A, Teesside

Dear Mr Seed,

I am nineteen years of age and I just wanted to write to you to say how much I enjoyed reading your book. You've put the thought into my mind to stop my stupid behaviour and grow up before it's too late.

I don't normally read, but my cell mate told me all about it so I thought I'd give it a try and out of a scale of one to ten, it would definitely be a ten. It's amazing how you just turned your life around. Hopefully I'll be as lucky as you.

Thank you

P, Doncaster

Hi Gram,

I have just read your book and I liked it a lot. I could relate to it a lot because I have been on drink and drugs since I was twelve years old and been coming to jail since I was fifteen years old. I have become a Christian and I am ready to make a big change in my life. I would really like to go to the halfway house you talk about at the end of the book. I like the whole idea of it and I am really interested. I hope you are coming in here to see us soon.

J, Teesside

Dear Gram,

I just read your book and I must say it was a fantastic insight into your life. It was like I was reading about myself in many ways and I had a lump in my throat reading it, as I am a man that had it all and lost it all. My faith in God is great and I believe everything happens for a reason; it's how we come through the other side that makes us men.

I know there's a beautiful life ahead if I give myself to the Lord, but Gram I must say I am scared by the change. I know I must accept his love and turn my life around as I have seen the dark side. I don't want that, I want redemption with God's love. I know I must embrace it and have the courage to fulfil my time positively on earth as great things lay ahead. God bless you, my friend, and may God be with you.

S, Bridgend

Dear Mr Gram Seed,

I've never before been compelled to write to anyone, never mind about my feelings and beliefs. I'm sure you've heard it all before the similarities I have with your story and it gave me great comfort, as for the first time in my forty-six years I do not feel alone.

After being released from prison I was in a position where my wife and two beautiful daughters were being threatened with eviction. Instead of being a man, I withdrew into drink and drugs to deal with it and was soon being treated for severe depression. This led to several pathetic attempts to take my life. During the last attempt, I slit my wrists and decided to leave the house and go to the woods where in my sick mind I thought my daughter would not find the mess and feel hurt.

I got ten yards, collapsed and was found, amazingly, three hours later in a place that was almost invisible from the road. My next memory was crying my eyes out in the ambulance and as I didn't want to be sectioned again, I lied my way out of hospital and was arrested for the possession of a knife.

I am now looking at an additional three years in prison, but I don't feel bitter or twisted as I just recently prayed to Jesus for help. I believe he answered me when I arrived in the prison and the chaplain put his hand on my shoulder, prayed for me and handed me your book. I've enrolled in his group and pray that this unexplained feeling of peace and hope stays with me.

So God bless you for the work you are doing and the book you wrote that answered questions in a very confused man's head.

Yours sincerely

H, Glasgow

BOOLA

A close friend of mine [Boola] said he's read loads of stories about Christians. He likes the first half of the book, but not the bit when they find God. He doesn't believe it and thinks lads in prison become Christians to get parole. But he told me if he ever read my book, he'd believe it, because he knows there's something different about me. He's seen it.

Gram Seed, *One Step Beyond*

Boola's response:
I was brought up with Gram – we came from the same violent upbringing. I know what Gram says is the truth and I truly believe that he found God and a better life. I didn't find God and now I'm doing 'life'. I can see in Gram's story the difference God has made in his life.
Sent from HMP Frankland

AND FINALLY, FROM THE MOUTHS OF BABES ...

I thought it was really good that Gram became a Christian. Lots of people can become Christians if they read his book. I think God makes a difference because sometimes you are bad and if you listen to God it can stop you being so silly.
Hannah Williamson (Ian and Rachel Williamson's daughter), aged 7

SOWING SEEDS MINISTRIES

Sowing Seeds Ministries is a Christian charity that exists to bring the love of Christ to prisoners and ex offenders. The charity has three main goals:

1. To bring hope to those in trouble with the law and help them find faith.
2. By helping them, so reduce crime.
3. To provide help and support for the families of people in prison; they also suffer.

The charity aims to raise enough funds, through individual donations and grants, to employ additional staff to assist with the ministry, find accommodation to serve as a halfway house for ex offenders and eventually purchase a farm to assist rehabilitation and teach employable skills.

For further information and to make a donation, please contact:

Sowing Seeds Ministries
PO Box 821
Stockton-on-Tees
TS19 1FD
United Kingdom

Telephone: 01642 575157; **mob:** 07983 382888
Email: info@sowingseeds.org.uk
Website: www.sowingseeds.org.uk
UK Registered Charity Number: 1118261
UK Registered Company Number: 6010713

A PERSONAL COMMENT ...

When I was invited to write a second book about Gram Seed, I hesitated. It had been a difficult year; at the time when *One Step Beyond* was inspiring hope and changing lives, mine was falling apart. How could I possibly write all these wonderful new stories when mine didn't appear to have a happy ending? Maybe I wasn't the right person for the project.

Working on the book came painfully close to home at times and all too often I seemed to be living what I was writing. That wasn't what I'd signed up for! But by doing what I believe God wanted me to do, there was also the richest of blessings – hearing about the way Gram's first book inspired so many readers, witnessing first hand the warmth, love and dedication of the Sowing Seeds team, meeting those with lives transformed through that love in action and enjoying the wonderful peace and hospitality offered at Gram's home with his lovely wife and family. I could have missed out on all that.

We also had the challenge of squeezing the creation of a book into two busy lives – often having to interview Gram and the team on the run, travelling between prisons, fitting phone calls around respective school runs and bedtime stories and reworking the manuscript in parks, play areas, cafés and a hospital ward! But as the book started to emerge, God continued to bless on many occasions, often using the material to encourage me personally; on one occasion, while working on Mike Gallagher's testimony, hours away from a particularly painful anniversary, God spoke to me using a verse Mike had quoted: 'Forget the former things; do not dwell on the past. See, I am doing a new thing!' (Isaiah chapter 43, verse 18). God's perfect timing.

It has truly been a privilege to be involved in both of these projects. I pray that *It Must be Love* has blessed and encouraged you as much as it has me and helped to bring home the vital truth that no matter what situation you are in, if you 'trust in the Lord and do good', He can turn your life around, help you find purpose through the pain and ultimately, give you 'beauty for ashes'.

God bless you
Andrea Robinson

NATIONAL DISTRIBUTORS

UK: (and countries not listed below)
CWR, Waverley Abbey House, Waverley Lane, Farnham, Surrey GU9 8EP.
Tel: (01252) 784700 Outside UK (44) 1252 784700

AUSTRALIA: KI Entertainment, Unit 31 317-321 Woodpark Road, Smithfield, New South Wales 2164. Tel: 02 9604 3600 Fax: 02 9604 3699

CANADA: David C Cook Distribution Canada, PO Box 98, 55 Woodslee Avenue, Paris, Ontario N3L 3E5. Tel: 1800 263 2664

GHANA: Challenge Enterprises of Ghana, PO Box 5723, Accra.
Tel: (021) 222437/223249 Fax: (021) 226227

HONG KONG: Cross Communications Ltd, 1/F, 562A Nathan Road, Kowloon.
Tel: 2780 1188 Fax: 2770 6229

INDIA: Crystal Communications, 10-3-18/4/1, East Marredpalli, Secunderabad – 500026, Andhra Pradesh. Tel/Fax: (040) 27737145

KENYA: Keswick Books and Gifts Ltd, PO Box 10242-00400, Nairobi.
Tel: (254) 20 312639/3870125

MALAYSIA: Salvation Book Centre (M) Sdn Bhd, 23 Jalan SS 2/64, 47300 Petaling Jaya, Selangor. Tel: (03) 78766411/78766797 Fax: (03) 78757066/78756360

Canaanland, No. 25 Jalan PJU 1A/41B, NZX Commercial Centre, Ara Jaya, 47301 Petaling Jaya, Selangor. Tel: (03) 7885 0540/1/2 Fax: (03) 7885 0545

NIGERIA: FBFM, Helen Baugh House, 96 St Finbarr's College Road, Akoka, Lagos.
Tel: (01) 7747429/4700218/825775/827264

PHILIPPINES: OMF Literature Inc, 776 Boni Avenue, Mandaluyong City.
Tel: (02) 531 2183 Fax: (02) 531 1960

SINGAPORE: Alby Commercial Enterprises Pte Ltd, 95 Kallang Avenue #04-00, AIS Industrial Building, 339420. Tel: (65) 629 27238 Fax: (65) 629 27235

SOUTH AFRICA: Struik Christian Books, 80 MacKenzie Street, PO Box 1144, Cape Town 8000. Tel: (021) 462 4360 Fax: (021) 461 3612

SRI LANKA: Christombu Publications (Pvt) Ltd, Bartleet House, 65 Braybrooke Place, Colombo 2. Tel: (9411) 2421073/2447665

USA: David C Cook Distribution Canada, PO Box 98, 55 Woodslee Avenue, Paris, Ontario N3L 3E5, Canada. Tel: 1800 263 2664

For email addresses, visit the CWR website: www.cwr.org.uk
CWR is a Registered Charity – Number 294387
CWR is a Limited Company registered in England – Registration Number 1990308

Day and Residential Courses
Counselling Training
Leadership Development
Biblical Study Courses
Regional Seminars
Ministry to Women
Daily Devotionals
Books and Videos
Conference Centre

Trusted all Over the World

CWR HAS GAINED A WORLDWIDE reputation as a centre of excellence for Bible-based training and resources. From our headquarters at Waverley Abbey House, Farnham, England, we have been serving God's people for over 40 years with a vision to help apply God's Word to everyday life and relationships. The daily devotional *Every Day with Jesus* is read by nearly a million readers an issue in more than 150 countries, and our unique courses in biblical studies and pastoral care are respected all over the world. Waverley Abbey House provides a conference centre in a tranquil setting.

For free brochures on our seminars and courses, conference facilities, or a catalogue of CWR resources, please contact us at the following address.
CWR, Waverley Abbey House, Waverley Lane, Farnham, Surrey GU9 8EP, UK

Telephone: **+44 (0)1252 784719**
Email: **mail@cwr.org.uk**
Website: **www.cwr.org.uk**

CWR Applying God's Word
to everyday life and relationships

From mayhem to ministry – a life transformed

Effective evangelism tools

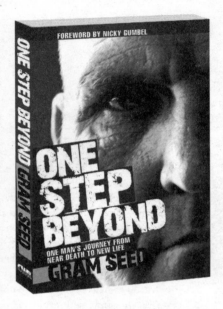

If you enjoyed *It Must be Love*, you will want to read Gram Seed's autobiography *One Step Beyond*.

Take a faith-boosting journey with Gram as he goes from a life of crime and addiction to helping others find new life in God's kingdom.

Your confidence in God's ability to change lives will increase as Gram tells of his miraculous recovery from a six-day coma and how, with the strength of his new-found faith, he started helping other young offenders find God's amazing love and forgiveness.

ONE STEP BEYOND

by Gram Seed
ISBN: 978-1-85345-462-2
£7.99

Eye-opening docu-drama

Gram Seed's story is powerfully told in this 34-minute DVD featuring re-enactments of Gram's life of crime, addiction, hospitalisation, redemption, recovery and ministry.
Includes interviews and testimonies.

ONE STEP BEYOND DVD

EAN: 5027957001084
£9.99

Prices correct at time of printing and exclusive of p&p

One Step Beyond comic pack

This pack contains five copies of Gram's story retold in an eight-page, full-colour, graphic-novel-style comic.
This simplified version covers Gram's life from football hooliganism, through jail, drugs, drink and a six-day coma, to his miraculous recovery as God entered his life.
Ideal for use at evangelistic events, prisons, drop-in centres, youth groups etc.

FROM NEAR DEATH TO NEW LIFE (A4 graphic story)

ISBN: 978-1-85345-494-3
£4.99 for a pack of 5
Price correct at time of printing and exclusive of P&P